With Radiant Hope

Timely and Timeless Reflections from George W. Truett

George W. Truett

Edited by Todd D. Still
with Scott M. Gibson

BIG BEAR BOOKS

Baylor University Press and the editor wish to express gratitude
to Scott M. Gibson and Dan Gregory for their part in making this
project possible.

Book design by Kasey McBeath
Cover design by *the*BookDesigners
Cover art courtesy of Shutterstock/Gajus and Valeriya_Dor

Hardcover ISBN: 978-1-4813-1399-5
Library of Congress Control Number: 2020941716

Dedicated to the memory of

Dr. James W. Vardaman

(1928–2018)

Contents

Foreword

Todd D. Still

O ne of the traditions that has arisen over the course of the relatively brief history of Baylor University's George W. Truett Theological Seminary is an annual Christmas banquet for current students, faculty, and staff.[1] One of the traditions that has developed within this tradition is for Brian C. Brewer, Professor of Christian Theology at Truett and the seminary's first graduate, to read to banquet attendees in any given year one of the thirty-four extant year-end messages written by George W. Truett (1867–1944) to the people whom he pastored at First Baptist Church, Dallas, Texas, where he served as pastor from 1897 to 1944.

Earlier this year, Scott M. Gibson, Professor of Preaching, suggested to me that it would be good if Truett's year-end messages were more widely known and circulated. To that good end, Dr. Gibson's graduate assistant and a student in the seminary's Ph.D. in Preaching program, Dan Gregory, recently supplied me with PDFs of Truett's now out-of-print, year-end messages, originally published as *These Gracious Years* (New York: Richard R. Smith, Inc., 1929) and *Christmas Messages* (Chicago: Moody Press, 1945), respectively.

Thereafter, I approached my colleagues at Baylor University Press, David Aycock and Cade Jarrell, to gauge their interest in publishing a volume combining the two works. Due to their receptivity, the rest, as they say, is history.

While tempting, this is not the place to consider George W. Truett's influential life and ministry or to assess his place in ecclesial history.[2] A few introductory remarks about what one finds herein, however, may prove to be valuable to readers of this volume.

With Radiant Hope is a collection of thirty-four year-end messages that George W. Truett wrote to his congregation while serving as pastor of First Baptist Church, Dallas. The messages span the years 1910 to 1944. During this timeframe, World War I (1914–1918), the Spanish Flu pandemic (1918–1920), the Great Depression (1929–1933), and World War II (1939–1945), to name but four herculean challenges encountered by Truett and his congregation, occurred.

Additionally, during this time period, Truett served as a preacher to Allied forces during the First World War (1918), delivered his famous address on "Baptists and Religious Liberty" on the steps of the Capitol in Washington, DC (1920), and served as President of the Southern Baptist Convention (1927–1929), President of the Baptist World Alliance (1934–1939), and as a Trustee of Baylor University (1934–1939), the school from which Truett graduated with his A.B. in 1897 (after having previously helped to save the school from certain financial ruin).

Although Truett does not typically mention contemporary events or his involvements external to the church in the course of his year-end messages, such are occasionally spoken of explicitly and frequently lurk in the background.

Additionally, while no two messages are precisely the same, Truett's year-end, pastoral missives possess a similar structure, style, and substance.

Truett typically begins his Christmas and New Year messages to his congregants with a similar and familiar well-wish. Thereafter, he usually offers the assembly an extended wish-prayer. In closing, he almost always places in front of his people an encouraging word regarding "the land where no shadow ever falls."

Similarities notwithstanding, there are discernable differences between the messages. One superficial difference is that Truett's letters to his people grew longer over time; one substantive difference is that the pastor's letters grew more didactic over time.

Regardless of length and tack, the strength of these magnanimous communiqués from beginning to end is their pastoral tone, literary quality, biblical basis, and theological character. In what follows, you will be reading what Truett wrote. Occasionally, I will add a content note along the way to illumine or to elaborate upon certain aspects of the letters, not least quotations from and allusions to Scripture, hymnody, and literature.

There is, of course, no one right way to read the messages that comprise this volume. Some will want to read them straight through, perhaps in swift succession in a single sitting. Others, perhaps, will want to savor them, reading them one a day, or a handful a day, over a stretch of time. Beginning at Advent and continuing through Christmastide holds promise for being an especially meaningful way to use this book. Whatever the case, though situated at year's end, these letters are for all seasons and are valuably read again and again at any time.

Regardless of how this book is read, this collection of messages will help one to see why it was said of Truett that when he spoke people listened. The contention that George W. Truett was Texas Baptists' gift to the world may well be an exaggeration, but in my not-so-objective opinion, it is not much of one! In any event, please enjoy this volume and the voice behind it, which are teeming with radiant hope.

Waco, Texas
Summer 2020

An Introductory Word from
These Gracious Years[3]

It is a privilege to present the messages gathered together for this book, as they have come from the heart of Dr. George W. Truett in his pastorate through a long course of years. They were not written with any expectation of thus being presented in book form, but represented year by year, out of the circumstances then prevailing, the informal messages this pastor wished to send to his own people. They are presented without revision.

A look back over these seventeen years will show great changes in our national life and still greater changes in the life of the great city in which he preached. These messages fit themselves into this growing, enlarging, and constantly shifting period. They breathe the life of a section, a nation, and a world in the period covered; and there has never been a more interesting period.

To be understood, they must be read with this time element in mind. Not unnaturally, they also represent the maturing mind of their author. In seventeen years, one passes through various phases of natural human development. They represent, therefore, the mental, moral, and spiritual growth of this rarely useful preacher, who is at the same time a loving pastor. Throughout runs the one continuous strain of unfaltering confidence in the purposes of God, in the leadership of Jesus as the Divine King, and the personal ministry of the Holy Spirit. They tell of an unchanging gospel in a changing age.

These messages come from a heart of faith and will be welcomed for the ring of confidence and assurance which they bring to us all, not only as messages for Christmas time, but as messages for all the days of the year, as we live and love and labor.

I. J. Van Ness

Reflection 1

This marks the return of the glad season, when the heart's kindly wishes find their way to the lips in words. I am wishing you a Merry Christmas and a Happy New Year. My prayerful thought for you is that the day may be one of truest joy and the year one of unusual blessing—and that you may have many more such days and years—through all of which you shall fulfill the true purpose of life.

May you be so anchored to Him from whom all blessings come, that your every step may be crowned with the victorious sense of His love and guidance. And then when the day comes to meet the Unseen Pilot, may you meet Him unafraid, and go forever to be with Him and to be like Him, in that timeless, tireless, sinless, deathless land, where there shall be no more sunsets and no more night.[4]

Christmas 1910

Reflection 2

At this gladsome Christmastide, my fervent wish for you is that as the Old Year passes and the New Year begins, you may close the one and begin the other, with memories so joyous, hopes so heartening, and blessings so appropriate as to crown your present and future with inexpressible happiness and imperishable usefulness.

And may every succeeding year and day come to you radiant with hope,[5] bringing such experiences only as may be best for you. Whatever the experiences, may the unseen but Almighty helper, the Master of life and light and love, direct you by His counsel, and reinforce you for every duty, Himself ever journeying with you and speaking to you as a friend speaketh to a friend.[6]

And when your day's work is done, and the gathering shadows of the eventide deepen into nightfall, may you go to live with Him and with others whom you love, in the land where no shadow ever falls, and where His presence and theirs will crown you with perfect happiness forevermore.

Christmas 1911

Reflection 3

Comes the recurring Christmastide, when the Old Year is hastening into the past and a New Year is at its birth, and I am thinking of you and wishing you every best Christmas and New Year's blessing. And this wish I cherish for you, not merely for a day or a season, but always.

The prayer that I offer for myself is the prayer that I would fain offer for you:

Through all the sunshine and the shade of the untried days, may the Angel of His Presence go with you! May you be given wisdom to discern the true values of life, so that your powers may not be wasted on the things which are false and superficial and valueless, but consecrated to the things which are high and deep and true—to those things only which satisfy and help! In your quest for happiness, may you find it only where it can be found—in loving the Divine Friend whom you have not seen and in serving the human friend whom you have seen![7] May God's world here and now be better and lovelier because of you! May there be light for you at the evening time, when, for a moment, you are hushed to sleep! And may you wake in the Yonderland, forever to be with the Prince of Love and with others "loved long since and lost awhile!"[8]

Christmas 1912

5

Reflection 4

A t this joyous season of Christmas greetings and good wishes for the New Year, when the fragrance of gift-making and good will is being wafted everywhere, I should deprive myself of a pleasure if I failed to send you a gift—not of silver and gold—but a gift of the heart, expressed in this prayerful wish for you:

Whatever the needs and tasks that may now and henceforth be yours, may consciously sufficient wisdom and strength be given you for them all, and may the Master's spirit of duty and service ennoble all your days and deeds.

May you be saved from the false lure of every unworthy motive, and from seeking after those things which are neither safe nor satisfying. May you ever pursue with eagerness all that is right and true and useful, inspired continually by the consciousness that you are living to be helpful in every way possible, to all who need your help.

In the hurried succession of the oft-changing and fast passing earthly days, may the entire oversight of your life be under the controlling guidance of the unseen but ever present Friend, Who is infinite in might and wisdom and love, and Who is pledged to turn into triumph all the checkered experiences of those who lovingly accept His guidance.

And when the hour of sunset shall come, may there be no shadows for you, but only the dawn of the morning eternal, with its light and love and music and hope and call to ever enlarging blessedness, in the House of Life, prepared by the Master of Life, for His friends.[9]

Christmas 1913

Reflection 5

As we pass another annual milestone in the journey of life, I would send you my best salutations, not merely for this happy season, but also for all the days and duties before you.

How fast the annual seasons of special greetings and good will succeed one another! How the passing years hurry away! That matters not, if only we will rightly use them as they pass.

I would breathe this fervent prayer for you, even as I offer it for myself:

That you may clearly know what life is for, and ever be strong in right purpose and action.

That you may be given wisdom and strength to set a supreme valuation on the things that are true and right, the high and vital things, and not on the things that are false and trivial and disappointing.

That you may remember that the charmed life is the life of faithfulness to duty, lead where it will, cost what it may.

That you may increasingly know the blessedness of comradeship with the Son of Man, in the right kind of service for all mankind, especially for those most in need of sheltering defense and friendship.[10]

That you may be strengthened with the graces of courage and patience and hope and trust and considerateness, in all the upward climb of life, and that you may have a noble disdain for all that is petty and groveling and selfish.

That you may worthily magnify faith—faith in all mankind, in God who is infinitely great and good, in the eternal verities, in the greatness of unselfish service, beside which all else is secondary, and is impotent to satisfy the cry of the eternal in the human heart.[11] That you may meet every duty and experience of life as they ought to be met, and when the tired day is over, rest well, because you have wrought well.

And when the new morning comes, beyond the mist-veiled harbor, may beckoning hands both Divine and human summon you to the Father's House of Many Mansions, where eternal compensation is given for all the hurts of time, where all conditions are perfect, and where you shall be crowned forever with the Crown of Life.[12]

Christmas 1914

Reflection 6

B ecause I am your friend, let me on the return of the happy Christmas and New Year Season, send you the kindest greetings of friendship, with every best wish for your highest happiness and usefulness, always.

As we pass through these lingering hours of the Old Year and begin the New, let us devoutly pray that the spirit of the Angels' Song—"On earth peace, good will toward men"[13]—may soon become so regnant in all the vast family of humanity, that the nations will beat their swords into plowshares, and their spears into pruninghooks, and war will cease from the world forever.[14]

For you, as for myself, I would breathe the earnest prayer that you may ever remember what life is for, and be utterly unwilling to turn aside into the bypaths of ease and self-seeking. May your vision of duty be clear, and your purpose steadfast, to know the exquisite happiness of helping all the people you can, being highly resolved not to waste any gift of life on profitless things. May you live always for the best things, rather than the second best. May you be given the seeing eye, the hearing ear, the understanding heart, that you may not miss the deeper, larger, more vital things of life, and may escape the little, the narrow, the mean and the foolish. Whatever the pain that may pierce your heart,[15] may you always be able to trace the rainbow through the rain.[16] May you bring the power of an endless life to bear upon the motives and deeds of the earthly life, so that the little things of time, shall be made great and be invested with eternal importance. May you ever implicitly trust Him Who embodies and interprets the everlasting mysteries, and Who is Himself the Light and Wisdom and Refuge of mankind. And at the end of the earthly day, may He turn the blind alley of death into a thoroughfare, that leads not to the twilight, but to the Dawn and the Eternal Homeland.

Christmas 1915

Reflection 7

Since you are in my kindliest thoughts at this recurring anniversary of Joy and Good Will, of Love and Hope, of Happy Greetings and Hearty Congratulations, I send this little message to tell you that I am wishing for you and yours, all that is best and happiest and most useful, through all this gladsome season—and through all the Afterwhile.

I would fain offer these Prayerful Wishes for you:

That songful memories may gladden you, and conquering hopes inspirit you, and wide-flowing helpfulness attend all your days and deeds.

That you may squander no time on vain regrets, on idle reveries, on carking anxieties, but may ever be given the majestic virtue of courage to overcome obstacles, endure trying tests, relight extinguished fires, and toil on unreluctantly at tasks which are never done.

That you may be given joy to triumph over all sorrow, strength to sustain you in all weakness, light to drive away all darkness, music for the day of tears, and hope to make you valiant against all fear.

That the higher things may be yours—a cheerful spirit, a contented heart, a clear conscience, a sure faith, peace of mind, and that you may be given wisdom correctly to appraise life, not only in its outward sense, but especially in the inner, finer, deeper meanings.

That you may always desire and strive to be of positive help to all humanity, joyfully bearing their burdens, being patient with their mistakes, seeking by love to repair the awful hurts wrought by selfishness, and while treading such royal path, may you be unceasingly inspired with the consciousness that you are walking in the steps of the Great Master, whose test of life is service.

That you may constantly live as seeing Him who is invisible, your soul calm, hopeful and unafraid, even when the winds are wild and the storms seem cruel, because of your abiding trust in Him who is pledged to turn all the distemperatures of life into triumphs for His friends.

That as birds forsake the wintry North, and fly toward the South, singing as they seek a sunnier clime, so you may travel on to the Ageless Land, singing all the way thither.

That the light upon all your earthly way—whether the way wind up the hill or down, through smiling prosperity or black-robed adversity—may shine brighter and brighter unto that perfect day which brings all sadness to an end, and all joy to a consummation.

And at the end of your earthly way, may you find that it is not an end but a beginning–the passing from the veiled and shadowy glory of the temporal into the unveiled and real glory of the eternal—where life and goodness and home and love and hope and knowledge and service shall be forever glorified.

Christmas 1916—New Year 1917

Reflection 8

The Season's Greetings are herewith sent you and yours, in an hour calling for all the wisdom and heroism of which we are capable. We have reached the fateful time when stupendous forces are rapidly remaking the world.[17] In such hour, the urge is upon us, as never before, to build all life on the granite foundations of righteousness, to meet all life with a larger helpfulness and deeper tenderness, and continually to sing the angel symphony: "Glory to God in the Highest, on Earth Peace, Good Will Toward Men." Though the world is now in the shadows, let us face the coming days with the prayer that they may be filled with the water of gladness, if that will be best for us; and if some days must be filled with the water of grief, let us trustingly cleave to Him who can turn the water into wine.[18]

In this hour of incomparable imperatives, we need to see in a truer perspective than heretofore, what supremely concerns us and others, and vicariously to dedicate our best for humanity's safety and usefulness, both for today and the great tomorrow. Let us specially seek to cleanse our hearts of all arrogance and easily besetting selfishness, and to exemplify lives of simplicity, equity, lofty patriotism, and true neighborliness, remembering that the obligations of neighborliness are as wide as humanity. Let us be Good Samaritans to the wounded, and weak, and suffering, and unfriended, and to all mankind, so improving every opportunity to help others, as shall cause them to think of Him who went about doing good, and trusted in His Father with a perfect heart.[19]

As we confront the larger duties now challenging us, let us diligently intone our consciences to all the higher calls of life, realizing that fidelity, and not rank, is life's crowning objective; and that the self-seeking life is the negation of God, the maladjustment of existence, the suicide of greatness, the defeat of opportunity, and the downfall of the soul. In all our goings, may we be given the discerning mind, the sympathetic heart, the kindly face, the golden tongue, the benevolent hand. In our quest to solve the problems of life, let us not forsake the Master of Life for some dream, or phantom, or abstraction, but let us be confidingly anchored to that infinite and unforgetting Friend, finding in Him the answer to life's deepest searchings and the solution of its most baffling questions. Whatever comes, may we ever be able to find the rose that smiles in the storm, and to see the light that shines behind the clouds.

And when we shall have finished all the errands of God in this life, and have come to the river, where on this side is "Good Night," and on the other the welcome of the Eternal Morn, may He dispel all the shadows, and bring us and ours to that Better Country, where are no anguished hearts, where no tear dims the eye, and where severed friendships and sundered loves are to bask in reunion eternal.

Christmas 1917—New Year 1918

Reflection 9

P robably ere this reaches you the happy Christmas season will be near at hand. Because of my absence and
duties, I cannot this year, as in previous years, send you
my personal card with Christmas greetings.[20] Let me, in
this letter to the Church, voice my heart's best Christmas
and Christian wishes for you, family by family, and person by person. And you will please pass on such greetings
from me, to all connected in any way with our Church
activities, to the Sunday congregations, to the Sunday
School, including the Home Department and the blessed
little ones in the Cradle Roll Department; to all the dear
young people of the Unions and those associated with
them; to the Women's Auxiliary; to the Men's Brotherhood; to the Thursday evening gathering; and to all the
dear, dear friends in Dallas, in which characterization I
would include every man, woman and child in our goodly
city. Heaven's gracious blessings be upon you all! Go singing with the Angels of old: "Glory to God in the highest,
and on earth peace, good will toward men."

Christmas 1918

Reflection 10

As we come again to the gladsome Christmastide, may we, with renewed joyfulness and purpose, together sing the angel symphony, not simply for one day or season, but through all coming days: "Glory to God in the highest, and on earth peace, good will toward men." May the love which is forbearing and kind, which does not covet for self but lives for others, which believes the best of all and never despairs of any, rule ever in all our hearts.[21]

As we recall the checkered experiences of the unquiet and fateful years that have recently passed and are passing, may we be upheld by the consciousness of God's sure presence with us and His gracious purpose concerning us, and amid all the mysteries that remain unsolved, may we be trustful and patient, courageous and unafraid.[22] May He tinge with golden light the dark cloud of every sorrow, and by the power of His hidden life may we be enabled bravely to put away all our forebodings and unfaith and fears.

As we relate our lives to others, may we be always so related to them that our chief thought concerning them shall be, not how we may get pleasure, profit, honor, or advancement from them, for ourselves, but how we may do them good, give them happiness, put honor upon them, always regarding every person whom we meet as one to whom we are sent on an errand of love and service. May we be increasingly given the insight of love, that we may both understand and serve all humanity, in the spirit of Him who said: "I am among you as one that serveth."[23] And may we never forget that nothing is small that helps a human life.

As we address ourselves to all the tasks awaiting us, may we be given all needed wisdom and strength from above, our hearts continually girded by the assurance that our tasks are by divine appointment and are for the betterment of humanity everywhere. May we remember that all the higher joys of life come only by the imparting of our strength to those who need it. May we steadfastly refuse to be engrossed with little questions and selfish programs, where myriads of humanity plead for the guidance which is safe and for the sympathy which is practical. May not a day of our lives henceforth be loveless, but, beginning with our own circles, may we faithfully strive to bring in the reign of love throughout all the circles of human life.

As new memorials of our Savior's love confront us, may we be correspondingly sensitive to every call of duty and every cry of need. May our vision be clarified that we may see clearly, and our scales of value be adjusted that we may be correct in our judgments, and our emotions so regulated that we shall instantly shrink from doing wrong, and be promptly constrained to every act which is right and helpful. May He daily unveil to us the glory of our inheritance,[24] that we may see the greatness of our earthly vocation. As we face all the issues of the hidden future, may we do so in the confidence that He ever goes before and with His friends, and that in Him nothing can befall us but what shall be eventually for our highest good. May we do our work to the last with a wholesome joy, and love our loves with an added tenderness, because the days of earthly love are short. And when the evening times come, may the light of our Great Pilot greet us, and may He bring us to the roomy spaces of the House of Many Mansions, where, with Him and with our dear ones loved long since and lost awhile, we may live and love and reign forever.

Christmas 1919

Reflection 11

As we come again to the gladsome Christmas and New Year Days, when one's thoughts go wistfully out to his friends, let me send you a little gift, not a gift material, but a gift of the heart, even the prayerfully fervent wish that the highest meaning of both days may be yours in joyful and abundant measure.

At this happy holiday season, may you be constrained to sing anew the most grateful song—for home and loved ones of the hearthside, and for friends both old and new, and for all the tender links of sympathy and hope by which life is made so pleasureful and inspiring.

If some memories of wrong choices and ill-kept resolutions in the past give you pain, may you turn to the future with clarified vision, with loftier views of duty, with more patient fidelity, with renewed power for the acquisition of the things that are right and for the reprehension of the things that are wrong, and may all your future be illumined with the radiant colors of hope.

In all your relationships, may the way of duty be made plain, and may you have the will and the strength to walk therein at whatever cost. As the flowers unconsciously breathe their fragrance, so may you constantly radiate helpfulness and cheerfulness and righteousness and courage and faith, and thus may you continually repair the ravages wrought by selfishness. May you know that your vocation here is to strive to make a better world, to help to hush its sighing and swell its singing, to strengthen the chorus of peace and good will throughout all the earth.

Whatever may be the complexion of your varying circumstances, whether sorrow shall sometimes becloud your way, or disappointment make its keen thrusts, or temptation lay its attractive coils, may you ever turn faithfully to the Friend that sticketh closer than a brother,[25] and know the potency of His light and leading. May your trust in Him be sure, and then, may you rejoice that He who through the pathless sky dost guide the bird to its distant nest, will keep you in the circuit of His unforgetting love. And when your day's work is done, may He bring you to the land where all sorrow is brought to a final end and all joy to a perfect consummation.

Christmas 1920—New Year 1921

Reflection 12

That this may be the best Christmas and New Year Season that we have ever known, and that our noblest possible service may be given to make it the best in the home circle, social circle, and for all mankind, is my most fervent prayer for you and for myself, at this accustomed season for the expressions of good will.

In the present tumultuous, tremendous, incomparably fateful days, may we hark back to the message of the Christmas carol on the plains of Bethlehem: "Glory to God in the highest, and on earth peace, good will toward men." May our best memories be revived and our noblest hopes be relighted. May we be given the poise, the patience, the sympathy, the verve, the self-control, the courage, the loyalty and the faith, to walk unblenched and safely through the wildest storm, and to realize the triumphs that are unwasting and immortal.

Whatever the petty worries we may know, the trying situations, the perplexing questions, the sorrows that oppress and the surprises that poignantly pierce the heart, may all our ways be radiant with the insight of Faith, the triumph of Hope, and the resistlessness of Love. May we ever have a sublime contempt of all unfaithful ease, and all unfaltering fidelity to the majestic behest of duty. May we wage our most valiant warfare to be released from the tyranny of consuming anxiety, from the ignobleness of unworthy ambitions, and from the blighting defeats that inexorably follow selfishness. However harsh some facts of life may seem to be, may we realize that beneath all the bruises and heartaches there is an Omniscient Love that never fails, never forsakes, and never forgets.

May we clearly discern God's program for our lives, and trustfully hide ourselves within the ample purposes of His love and wisdom.

As we travel life's earthly road from Jerusalem to Jericho may we be good Samaritans to all who need us, cheering, healing and fortifying them with true neighborliness, vitalizing all the relations of life with an unselfish love, remembering that love is the strongest thing in the world—stronger than hate, stronger than evil, stronger than death. May we touch all life with the noble spirit of kindliest sympathy, dispensing good will everywhere. May we both diligently work and pray for the coming of that halcyon day when men shall beat their swords into plowshares and their spears into pruninghooks, when all discords and dissonance shall be done away forever; and may we see in God's love and purpose the only way of true fraternity for all mankind.

May the wistful call of the Eternal Tomorrow make us steadfast and faithful for the duties of today and for all the adventures of faith. And when we are called to stand beside the Silent Sea, and no human friend can journey with us on the Great Adventure, may we have an unfearing trust that our Great Companion Who died for us and has conquered death will deliver us from its sting and shadows forever.[26] And until the day break and the shadows flee away, may we with unbroken confidence yield our lives to the Light that followeth all our way, to the Joy that seeketh us through pain, and to the Love that will not let us go.[27]

Christmas 1921—New Year 1922

Reflection 13

As we come again to the glowing Christmas and New Year Season, the perennial reminder of the heaven-sent song and gift of peace and good will to all mankind, let it newly remind us how poor and formal our lives would be without our friends. Let us be highly resolved to make the gracious spirit of this joyful season a perpetual experience in all the relations of our lives.

As we approach the threshold of a New Year, let us do so with the fervent prayer and the unfaltering purpose to take with us all the Old Year held of instruction and triumph for us, and penitently leave all that it held of mistake and folly and regret, to be buried in the oblivion of God's forgiving grace.

Through every coming day, let us be alert to respond to every cry of need, and be unstinted in all friendly ministries toward everybody, everywhere, and always. Let us remember that it is not always by willful misdeed that we shut ourselves out of the circle of highest good, but often it is rather by the failure rightly to employ our passing opportunities to be a blessing unto others. Let us evade no call to be of service anywhere, to speak words of kindness everywhere, to impart our best strength and help forevermore, remembering that it was the unused talent, the unfruitful tree, the unhelpful life that the Great Master found worthy of sharpest reproof. Inasmuch as mutual service is the law of life, alike for the individual and for society, let us wisely give our utmost strength to correct everything that poisons the springs of confidence and good will, striving ever to walk in the steps of Him Who went about doing good. May nothing less than the best we can do for all mankind be satisfying to us, and may we unceasingly strive to live at the heights in spiritual nobleness, and may we never wander from the deep and healing shadow of His Cross.

Since the highest self-realization comes from the deepest self-sacrifice, let us put far from us that subtle vice which would tempt us to shun hardships and suffering. May our lives be freed from the slavery of selfish ease, from the misery of mean anxiety, from the unrest of unworthy ambition, and from the sorrows that come from grasping for ourselves.

If now and then the joys of life be turned into aching griefs—if there come to us haunting fears, and seeming ruthlessness, and silent defeats and nameless sorrows—let us keep looking for the bright light in the cloud, and trustingly follow Him with whom are the treasures that do not vanish and the joys that never cease to satisfy. Cleaving to Him who speaks the first word and the last, on Life and Death and the Eternal Beyond, let us meet every experience in quietness and confidence, forgetting never that even in life's darkest hours, standeth God within the shadows, keeping watch above His own. Let us fully accept His will as our will, our pillar of cloud by day and our pillar of fire by night, gladly giving ourselves into the keeping of Him who is the Way, the Truth, and the Life, and may we be found among His own, both for today and for the never-ending tomorrow. [28]

Christmas 1922—New Year 1923

Reflection 14

M ingled with the joyful chimes and friendly greetings of this happy Christmas and New Year Season are my thoughts of You—and to you and to yours, I am sending the twofold greeting: "A Merry Christmas and a Happy New Year."

At this gladsome Season, when all the world is brighter because of the Christmas gladness, and vocal with high resolves for the New Year and all the days ahead, let our steadfast purpose be to make the Christmas spirit perpetual and universal—to carry the Angels' Song of Glory, Peace and Good Will, everywhere, so that its three notes may ever increasingly become the marching music in every realm of the earthly life. Let us remember that the coming of the halcyon days when all the jarring discords of earth shall be hushed, will be hastened just in proportion as the spirit of this song shall become actually resident in our hearts, and the abiding principle of our lives.

If, at this songful Season some shadow is about us, because of some stinging disappointment, or some blinding sorrow—if some thorn, whatever it may be, has wounded the heart, let memory acutely remind us that a Heart of Infinite Love beats ever with changeless sympathy and goodness for our distraught and needy lives; and let us cleave to the Infinite Lover and Friend, with all the eagerness of our most loyal love, and trust Him with the expectation of unshaken confidence, remembering that the highest state of character is often reached by the way of sorrow. May the dews of our every sorrow be lustered by His love.

With our faces always toward the Sunrise, let us by the alchemy of faithful stewardship seek to transmute our every talent into noblest helpfulness for all mankind, recognizing that it is our majestic mission to link our human service with that of the Great Master, in spreading justice, mercy, peace and good will, not forgetting that He shall judge us, not by the prominence or the obscurity of our service, but by the faithfulness with which we perform it. May we wisely realize that every life, however humble, either increases or diminishes the sum total of human happiness, both for today and for the long tomorrow.

Let us evermore strive to keep out of our lives all cynicism and pessimism, all grudges and ill will, all misunderstanding and bitterness, all unintelligent and unfraternal intolerance; and let us constantly magnify the more tender virtues of gentleness, courtesy, kindliness, friendliness and serviceableness to all mankind. May we ever be keenly sensitive to the pathos of all human need, gladly proffering our friendship to the unfriended, our strength to the weak, our wisest and worthiest help to all.

Since our earthly life is so brief and precious, let us waste no time in striving after the things that can neither satisfy nor endure. Through all our earthly way, may we travel on with a steady faith, a victorious patience, a noble courage, so interpreting and using the privileges and relations God has given us as to make sure of a blissful immortality. More and more, may we know how good a thing is life, when it is lived in the reverent fear of God and in devotion to that which

He approves. And when we come to life's Sunset Hour, may
we be unafraid and ready to walk triumphantly through the
Valley of Shadows into the Land of Eternal Morning, to be
welcomed by our Friend Divine, and by our human friends
and loved ones, and to go out from His presence and theirs
no more forever.

Christmas 1923—New Year 1924

Reflection 15

During the golden Season of wistful memories and gracious wishes, of rejuvenated purposes and strengthened hopes, I would fain express the oft-repeated but never hackneyed greeting of friendliness and good will, for you and yours, not only for this returning Christmas and New Year Season, but also for all the unknown and unending future.

At this Wistful Season, when kindliest thoughts and most generous emotions are wont to be transformed into words and deeds, may we be given a more vital interest and practical sympathy for all mankind, and a deepened purpose to devote our every power in doing the largest good to all.

In these hurrying, auspicious days, may we learn more worthily how to appraise the true values of life, and realize more acutely, that the little things are often crowned with supreme significance. May we discern afresh the value of the friendly smile, the praiseful word, the grateful letter, the handclasp of confidence, the timely token, whatever it may be, that enkindles new purpose and inspiration in the lives alike of young and old. May we increasingly know that the staple of daily happiness is found in the small measures and common things of life.

As we confront the varied duties of our brief but eternally fateful earthly life, may we be given discerning wisdom to see what life is for and what its every duty means. May we make sure that life's essentials are secure with us, and that we care not too much for the subordinate. May we know that our serviceableness is to be as wide as the world and as enduring as human need; and that life cannot be seen in the crowning glory of its greatness and usefulness, until it is seen as a vicarious trusteeship, taking the place of a selfish individualism. May we therefore faithfully strive to meet life's every duty with undishonored fidelity, remembering that the use which we make of what we are and have is the final test of life.

Whatever may be the unfoldment of life's changeful ways for us, whether they be bright or dark, at ease or troubled, whether cheered by the companionship of cherished voices, or called to walk in a solitary way, may the surpassing charm of the good and true ever drive from us all attraction towards the evil and false. May we build all life genuinely and sincerely, utterly scorning to put one defective stone into the building. May we allow no bitterness or ill-will any lurking residence within our hearts; and may we steadfastly set ourselves against all unworthy intolerance and inhospitality, all bigotry and prejudice, all envy and detraction, all aloofness and suspicion, all misunderstandings and estrangements, remembering the blessedness of those who make peace between individuals and classes, here and there and everywhere.[29]

When suffering comes to us, may it always be an alchemist, consuming the dross and refining the gold, changing pride into modesty and self-seeking into sympathy. If sometimes called to moan in the silence, because of some haunting neglect or disappointed confidence, may we have the inviolable habit of looking for the silver lining of the cloud rather than its leaden gray. As birds of the sea sit singing upon the stormy waves, and are unafraid, because they can fly above the waves, so may we meet every experience unafraid, because we are guided and kept by an Omniscient Friend who sees and knows and cares. May we often seek a retreat from the glare of the garish day, to learn from Him the lore which is fit for living or dying or the immortal life. When the Grim Reaper passes by,[30] leaving a hush in the earthly home, may the infinite challenge of the Eternal Home help to calm and heal our hearts, till the night is gone, and the morning come, when we shall greet again the smiling faces which we have loved long since and lost awhile. Now and always, let us trustfully go on with Him whose Incarnate Wisdom can give the faith that casts out fear, the hope that defies despair, and the love that crowns all mortal life, and will live on, unmarred by death, throughout the Immortal Beyond.

Christmas 1924—New Year 1925

Reflection 16

This message is sent you, at this recurrent Christmas and New Year Season, to voice again for you and yours, the old-time greeting of friendliness and good will. Our swift-passing earthly life is made roseate by its friendships. No other human treasures can countervail one's friends.

May this joyful Season be the occasion for our most grateful reminiscence, and for our renewed devotion to home and friends and all the higher claims of life. Let us turn away from the Babel of contentious voices,[31] to catch again the message of the angel-choir: "Glory to God in the Highest, and on Earth Peace, Good Will Toward Men"; and let us henceforth seek, with unremitting devotion, to make this message the universal anthem of mankind.

Since the greatest things are always the summation of the smallest, let us individually and ever strive to enthrone the law of kindness in the home, courtesy in society, honesty in business, fairness in work, pity toward the unfortunate, help toward the weak, resistance toward unrighteousness, forgiveness toward the penitent, congratulation toward the fortunate, and reverent love toward God.

As we pause for a moment, at this Golden Season, before passing to the days and duties ahead, let us be highly resolved to forget all that we should not remember, and to remember all that we should not forget. May our coming days be crowned with a finer insight, a saner judgment, a more thoughtful considerateness, a more passionate sincerity, a more granite loyalty, a more practical serviceableness. May we know how to meet disappointment without resentment, and to be tolerant without being arrogant or unfaithful, remembering that clear thinking is atrophied by bitterness and intolerance and prejudice.

Let us labor unceasingly to bring all the happiness we can to others, and to bring them no unhappiness, foreseeing that when we come to life's last earthly hour, it will not be our kindness or patience or benevolence that we shall regret, but our harshness and neglect and our unfaith. Likewise, may we know that we do not have to be rich, or high-placed, or powerful, to be happy and to make others happy, but the secret is in persistent words and deeds of invincible good will; and that it is a paradox of life that by hoarding love and happiness and any and every talent, we lose them, and that only by giving them away can we keep them for ourselves.

In a world torn by lacerating words and unseemly strifes, let us dedicate ourselves, with wholehearted and unresting toil, to the task of creating and spreading the spirit of fraternal righteousness and constructive helpfulness, knowing that vicarious love can heal all wounds and bring all peoples into the glad acknowledgment of brotherhood, and into the mutual service which this acknowledgment implies.

Whether our unfinished journey shall be among dangerous rocks, or in the calm of the open sea, may we gladly choose that He Who came to give us the more abundant life,[32] shall decide for us how much of prosperity and happiness we may safely have; and if He must chasten us, may He graciously remember how little we can bear alone. May we be utterly unwilling to fortify ourselves with a fleeting happiness, and miss the enduring joys. May we wisely discern that the supreme disaster is to sacrifice the things that endure for the things that perish. May the vision and power of the world eternal attend all the problems and duties of our world temporal.

As we sometimes peer through the Westward Windows, and think of our passage through the Sunset Gate, let us unfearingly trust ourselves to Him Who guides the birds in their long and uncharted migrations, and Whose purpose in coming to earth, in the long ago, was to be the Way and Truth and Life and Light and Love for our needy world. Thus following Him, we shall arrive, at the Morning Gate, in His good time, to live forever with Him, and with all who are willing to be His friends.

Christmas 1925—New Year 1926

Reflection 17

As we stand at the portals of another Christmas and New Year Season, when the Carols of Joy and Peace and Good Will fill all the air, let me voice for you and yours, as for myself, the prayerful wish that the larger meanings of the old-time Christmas Carols may be more deeply written in our own and other lives, today, and through all days to come.

At this accustomed Season, when old friendships are renewed and new ones cemented, let us sing anew our most grateful song: that our lives have been planted in such a joyful fellowship of kindred life, with its wondrous power to gladden and uplift; for our homes and loved ones, for our friends and friendships, for the high privileges of thought and health and work; and for our highest welfare, both for today and the long tomorrow, at the hands of Infinite Love.

While the Old Year goes and the New Year comes, may we be highly resolved that no bitter thoughts and cynical complaints, no poisonous seeds of discord and ill will, shall be carried with us into the challenging days ahead; that nothing petty or groveling shall mar our future plans and deeds; that we will henceforth be courageously inhospitable toward that which harms mankind, and aggressively cooperative with that which helps; and that we will ever seek to leaven all the circles of life, with the spirit of the Golden Rule.[33]

When transfiguring visions are given us on the mountain heights, may we hasten to the vales below, where human lives and humanity-lifting causes send forth their poignant plea for our worthiest help.[34] May we wisely discern that all life's talents are given us, not for ourselves alone, but also in trust for others, and that such talents will surely work for our disaster, if we fail to employ them in unselfish service. May we acutely realize how vast a trust is our earthly life, and that its twelve brief hours shall soon be gone. May we diligently strive to fill all these hours with thinking serene and high; to do all our work with unfaltering fidelity and good cheer; to be worthily mindful of all who journey with us; and so to devote our lives in altruistic and sacrificial service, that our work shall live on beyond the day when our voices shall be hushed into the last silence. Likewise, may we realize that the tragedy of life is not poverty, pain nor hardship, but it is the shallow and dilettante interest in the highest objectives; that only by obedience to life's crowning purposes can life be abidingly happy and useful, and be finally saved from the tormenting memory of unaccepted responsibility; and that this is the only way whereby life's sunny days may be made enduring, and its cloudy days endurable.

If in our cup shall be mixed both joy and sorrow, prosperity and adversity, may we emerge from all our ways, like gold from the refiner's fire. May our steadfast faith in the Changeless Friend keep us undismayed and unembittered, amid all the mysteries and bludgeonings that may attend our journey. May every disappointment turn into blessing, and every care uplift us as with wings. And, as we go on, may we be sure that around our incompleteness flows His greatness, round our restlessness His rest, and that nothing but our own willfulness shall ever separate us from His encompassing love.[35] May we avoid the easy error of placing first things second, and wisely see that Eternity and Time are so inseparably blended, that both are to be faithfully reckoned with, if we are wisely to interpret either. If our hearts are sometimes sick from hope deferred;[36] if burdens are sometimes laid upon us which test our own faith and strength, if dark anomalies arise which are beyond our ken, may we refuse to waste one hour in futile worries, in vain regrets, in idle dreams, but may we be true to the highest light we have, till brought through battle smoke and weltering struggle to life's final Sunset.

Until the final Sunset comes, may all be well with us and ours, through all the coming, changeful days. And when the Sunset fades to Dark, and we are called to say "Good Night" to those we love, may fears be gone, because the Dark shall quickly break to Dawn. And with the Morning Light, may we go above, from the Land of Loss to the Land of Love, where Love shall ever have its own, in that ampler Home where fondest dreams come true, where Life shall be commensurate with its deepest longings, and where we shall ever live on in highest service.

Christmas 1926—New Year 1927

Reflection 18

L et me send you a gift, even such as I have to give, at this
Golden Christmas and New Year Season. The gift is a
Wish, with the deepest and highest meaning that can be
expressed by the old, old Greeting: "A Merry Christmas and
A Happy New Year."

The age-old Benediction would I also voice for you,
with all the fullness of gladness and blessing that can be
expressed by the blessed trinity of words: "God Bless You!"
Whatever may be your experiences, now and forever—
"God bless you!"

As this Festival Season comes again, freighted with the
exquisite fragrance of Gladness and Good Will, let us sing
with the Angels at Bethlehem, our most grateful Songs,
for the Divine Goodness which has attended our Past, and
which, we are glad to believe, will go with us into the Future
that waits veiled before us.

When we look upon a World confused and discordant,
and hear its poignant cry for sympathy and service, let
us joyfully hark back to the one adequate remedy for the
solution of all the problems of mankind, as announced in
the Chorus from the Choir Invisible: "Glory to God in the
Highest, and on Earth Peace, Good Will toward Men!"

May we eagerly hail this Mystic Season as the timely occasion for the renewal of friendships old, and for questing after

friendships new, by the worthiest possible radiation of the Spirit of Friendliness and Good Will, here, there, and everywhere. In the home circle, and with neighbors and friends, and toward all humanity, may it be our unwavering and most positive effort, today and hence, forth, to make life richer, sweeter, safer, happier and better, for every human being in the world.

With ever increasing alertness, let us seek to be delivered from the folly of a narrow outlook on life, and from the selfishness which shuts out Divine light and human need. If sometimes tempted to cling with selfish grasp to the little we have, of time, or property, or life, may the effective admonition come quickly to remind us that to hoard life selfishly is to lose it, and to give it unselfishly is to save it. May we wisely understand that the only way of abiding happiness and usefulness is found by walking in the steps of Him who said: "I am among you as He that serveth."[37]

As we turn our faces to the days and tasks ahead, may we do so with buoyant step, as into a land where larger happiness and usefulness await us. May we wisely forget every vestige of censoriousness, vindictiveness, cynicism, uncharitableness, and every other ugly passion. With equal diligence, may we exalt every call of graciousness, magnanimity, hopefulness, faithfulness, and every other handsome passion. May we ever think of others, not as selfish competitors whom we should hinder, but as creative cooperators whom we should help.

Let us face the future with purpose fixed to learn its lessons with humility; to meet its responsibilities with resolute will; to bear its crosses with patient hope; to be absolutely just and generous in all life's relations; to be too busy with the highest duties to remember injuries, and too magnanimous to cherish bitterness; to seek to keep the relations among all classes both equitable and beneficent; and to see to it that neither tradition nor prejudice shall transform convictions into unworthy intolerance.

If we must sometimes eat our bread in tears,[38] may we remember that it is through suffering and renunciation that all the finer qualities of life are evoked. May we be able to sing when the clouds lower, when fortune frowns, when the tides are adverse, remembering that a dauntless spirit is the way of triumph, both for ourselves and comrades. If we grow weary in our toiling, discouraged in our suffering, perplexed in life's crisis hours, may we never grow rebellious under a discipline which now we cannot understand. Always and everywhere, may we steadfastly think on the things that are great and fruitful and eternal, rather than those that are petty and barren and transient.

As citizens of two worlds, may we be given that broad view of life that comprehends its completeness, rather than the narrow view that magnifies its fragments. May we wisely realize that life has higher ranges of service and achievement than can be measured by the mortal; and that the fullness of life is impossible if our thoughts and aims and endeavors are limited to the temporal. As children are joyful and unafraid, when conscious that they are surrounded and guarded by watchful love, so may we go on with unfearing trust in the Great Pilot, gladly choosing that He shall be our all-sufficient help and hope, in life, in death, and throughout the vast Beyond forever.

Christmas 1927—New Year 1928

Reflection 19

L et all men hail again the brightness and gladness of the
magic Christmas and New Year Season, when the heart
is given larger sway, when neighbors become more neigh-
borly, and when strangers become friends.

At this wistful Season, with its added touch of thoughtful tenderness and radiant cheer, let me send you the age-
old greeting: "A Merry Christmas and a Happy New Year."
Let me also earnestly voice for you and yours, the prayerful
wish that is offered for me and mine, that an overflowing
measure of Joy and Peace may now befortune you, and that
God's best benison may go with you, throughout this joyous
Season and all the days that follow. As you journey on, may
you find hospitable Wayside Inns, all along the road of life,
where your thirst shall be refreshed by tokens of noblest
friendliness which you shall both receive and give; and may
the Omniscient Friend ever set upon your board the plate
of sufficient plenty and the cup of sustaining cheer.

At this glad Season for happy memories, high resolves,
and beckoning visions, let us summon ourselves to listen
anew to the old-time Song of the Angels: "Glory to God in
the Highest, and on Earth Peace, Good Will toward Men,"
which Song is steadily changing all life from dismal thren-
ody into triumphant jubilation. Let us worthily realize that
the poignant needs of our troubled world are not causes

for despair, but they are challenges to our compassion and chivalry and wisdom and fidelity. May we ever be given wise and busy hands to enthrone the law of peace among all humankind, to overthrow all injustice, to banish the spirit of unmercifulness, to put away all hopelessness, to turn all ill will out of the house of life, and to enthrone the spirit of good will, everywhere.

As the Calendar of the untraveled future unfolds before us, may we be profoundly aroused from all reluctance to do our full part in helping all humanity to a larger chance, to a better condition, to a happier and more useful life, ever consecrating our best for the common burden and the public trust. May our dominant motive in life be that of cooperative altruism instead of selfish individualism. May we be utterly unwilling to miss the strength that comes from burden bearing, or the joy that comes from the hard-fought battle. May we deliberately choose the task which most taxes our highest powers and which best serves humanity's deepest needs. May we deeply realize that there is no prosperity that is not founded on right living, and that no permanent gain can come to any one from what occasions another's loss.

As we turn from the past to the future, may the memories of yesterday bring oil to the lamp of our hopes for all the days ahead. May we wisely leave behind all that would mar our peace and progress, and carry forward only that which would make life happier and better for ourselves and others. May we be given the instructed conscience which leads to right decisions; the self-control we need in the hour of provocation; the hope we need in the presence of uncertainty; the patience we need to endure the buffetings of life; the forbearance we need in dealing with others; the vision we need of life's essential and supreme things; and the wholehearted spirit that would spend all in their worthy achievement.

Through all coming days, may there be such unity in our purposes as shall blend the temporal and spiritual in such a way as to glorify the whole life. If some days shall be marked by adversity and others by prosperity, may we not be embittered by the one nor coarsened by the other. Let us not grumble at the chilly winter if it helps to bring out the flowers and fruits of the gracious summer. May we be lifted above the pessimism which magnifies the shadows and be fortified by the optimism which sees the way of life as the shining light which shineth more and more unto the Perfect Day. If times of poignant loneliness shall come, when we sigh for the touch of a hand that has vanished and the sound of a voice that is still, may both Memory and Hope remind us of the Kindly Light that is leading us to a Land where Love has its eternal habitations, the Father's House of Many Mansions, the final, eternal home for all who would be won by His love. May we wisely realize that we are now in training for that Better Land, where with perfect conditions we are to learn and grow and love and serve forever.

Christmas 1928—New Year 1929

Preface from *Christmas Messages*[39]

Yielding to the requests of friends who felt the absence of Doctor Truett's Christmas message last year, and remembering the generous welcome accorded the little volume published in 1929, *These Gracious Years*, consisting of previous messages from his heart to the hearts of his friends, I have been impelled to compile the messages sent out since 1928.

This is done with the hope that this little book may bring comfort, help, and inspiration to those who need friendship and an uplifting thought, at the Christmas time.

These messages are timeless and are as true today as they were the day they were written.

May God's blessing rest upon each of you who read them, and may he who has gone yet speak to your heart with his words of comfort and cheer and lead you along paths of righteousness for His name's sake.

Mrs. Geo. W. Truett
Dallas, Texas

Reflection 20

A t this Holiday Season of dear comradeship with those who are near, and of joyful recollection of those who are far away, and of inexpressibly tender memories of those who have gone within the veil, let us wisely remember that without these, life would be barren and hopeless, even though we had all else.

At this time let us joyfully sing our worthiest Song of Gratitude—for home and for friends; for the breath of life, the power to think, and the skill to work; for the temporal blessings which supply our real needs, and for the discipline of toil and of sorrow; for every acid experience which dissolves an unworthy intolerance and an unsympathizing indifference; for the visions which beckon us to honor and service, and for the glory of struggle and adventure; for the increasing purpose of Peace and Good Will running through the years, and for the confident hope that the Song of the Angels of the First Christmas Dawn shall one day echo and re-echo through all the earth; and, above all, for the Kindly Light that leads us, and for the Love that never forgets us, and for the Mercy that heals our hurts and lifts us when we fall.

Upon entering the gateway between the Old Year and the New, let us go forward, indomitably hopeful, resolutely striving to put away all joylessness and pessimism and unkindliness, and every tincture of selfishness, wisely remembering that no abiding joy nor permanent profit to ourselves can ever be purchased at the expense of others. May we be inexorably unwilling to give any place in our lives to rankling discords, to unseemly nor malign contentions, being always aware that life is too brief and great and responsible, to waste one minute of it in bearing that heaviest of all burdens—a grudge. May the constructive and graciously benevolent spirit of our lives help to overcome the rudeness and harshness and disharmonies of our discordant world, and may all our coming days be days of invincible Good Will. May we also be given such a full-orbed sensitiveness as will instantly respond to all the needs which vibrate in the whole range of human life. Let us fully apprehend that it is a mocking tragedy for life to be lived in ignorance of the joy of generous giving; that to keep happiness, it must be given away; that to lift another's load is to lighten our own; and that as the waters fled away from Tantalus, do all the higher, nobler things of life flee away from the self-seeking spirit.[40]

Through all the unfolding future, may we never forget that the nobly creative and conquering hours cannot come to the life that is occupied by petty ambitions and tawdry enterprises. May we continually meet the challenge of our daily task in the glowing spirit of creative achievement, and never in the spirit of the drudge or the shirk; and may we ever shun the shame of the second best. In the lowliest toil, the most unwelcome duty, the task that bristles with difficulty, the grey disappointment, the black sorrow, may we see the clear light of an infinite purpose, and feel the sufficient inspiration of an Eternal Love.

If our ways, at times, shall be shadowed by poignant tests, may our sorrows be wise teachers, our disappointments needed revelations, and our temptations victorious helpers toward a better life. If sometimes we think ourselves ill-treated by some person or cruel circumstance, may we never become cynical or vindictive. If we must sometimes travel in the darkest night, without sheen of moon or gleam of stars, may we never forsake our obedience to the highest visions. Whatever the tests of our earthly way, may they be borne with a fortitude which no reverses can daunt and with a faith which no trials can discourage. Ever let us know that He who does not allow a sparrow fall unheeded, counts us of more value than many sparrows.[41]

In all the diversity of our checkered experiences, may we trustfully turn to Him, in Whom are all the treasures of knowledge and wisdom,[42] and all the peace and power of the victorious life. Let us steadfastly refuse to travel blindly on, without adequate light, either on the meaning of this life or the next, and may we attune our lives and work to the rhythm of the Immortal Life. When our earthly day is ended and our work is done, may the gathering shadows of the evening be quickly merged into the Dawn of the Eternal Morning, and may we awake in that fair Morning, to be joyously greeted by our loved ones, and by Him whose love is unimaginably great, and in His likeness and presence be forever satisfied.

Christmas 1929—New Year 1930

Reflection 21

As the South Wind comes from sunny seas, driving away the cold and ice and snow, so comes again the joyous Christmas and New Year Season, driving away our defeats, neglects, and disappointments. At such Season, all are constrained, afresh, to drink deeply at the fount of friendliness and good will. It is preeminently the Season when the heart stirs with desire to cement friendships old, and to form friendships new. You will, therefore, generously allow my heart to have the right of way, and send you, by this little card, the perennial greeting: "A Merry Christmas and a Happy New Year," with the added bundle of good wishes for you and yours, that I am making for myself and mine.

At this Golden Season, when we look both backward and forward, may the veil of ingratitude be lifted from our eyes, and clear vision be given us of the unceasing and adequate blessings which have attended all our yesteryears, and which now crown our lives. Let us seek to be worthily grateful for our home life, with its measureless ministries of mutual understanding and affection; for the joyful inspiration that is continually given us by our friends; for the life that we are privileged to share with our fellow humanity; for Memory that enables us to relive the happy past; and for Hope that forecasts and seeks the ultimate enthronement of Peace and Good Will, throughout all the world.

As mariners examine the compass of their ships, before they venture upon the unvoyaged deep, so may we faithfully seek to examine every unworthy habit and standard of our lives, as we travel on into the unfolding future, not knowing whether our journey shall be among the dangers of the hidden rocks, or in the open seas. May we turn resolutely away from the mistakes and errors of the past, and with purpose worthy and faith unfaltering, go steadfastly on in the path that shineth more and more unto the Perfect Day. May we cast into the deep oblivion of forgetfulness every memory of any ingratitude or unkindness toward us, of any friendship shattered or unrequited, or of any ill-meant wound, and cast out of our lives all traces of bitterness and ugly suspicion. May we put far from us the cynical spirit, the censorious tongue, and refuse utterly to engage in hurtful gossip, or to listen to it. May we be ever given the vision which finds the major values of life, the courage which refuses to accept any defeat as final, the love which seeketh not its own, the hope which sees the dawn beyond the dark.

Let us persistently refuse to allow our lives to be cluttered up with things that make but little difference, but consistently give our unyielding emphasis to the vital, central, supreme things, wisely remembering that the chiefest things are often unveiled in the most commonplace duties. May we count it life's highest duty and privilege to translate all our powers into assets with which to help others less privileged than ourselves. May we never allow ourselves to look upon any human life cheaply, nor to lose our faith in the marvelous possibilities of the humblest life, for the noblest attainments. Let us remember that humanity is bound together in the bundle of life, and that we cannot ignore our duty to anybody.

May we faithfully realize that altruistic cooperation, rather than selfish competition, is both the norm and the goal of the well-ordered life; that we may easily become pettily provincial, and live in some Sleepy Hollow,[43] and allow small and selfish trivialities to cause us to miss the larger, more worthwhile things of life; that the constantly growing inter-dependence of human life everywhere, ever increasingly constrains to a better understanding and a closer cooperation among all classes, for the wisest of reasons—personal, social, economic, governmental, educational, moral, and religious. Let us also realize that the hope of the world for the ending of war, for the furtherance of good will, and for lasting peace, depends upon individual initiative and effort, and that every Bastille of discord and tyranny and selfishness must go down before the advancing march of peace and righteousness and worthy cooperation.

In our laudable desire to live happy lives, let us wisely remember that happiness is a byproduct of giving, and not of getting; that happiness and selfishness do not grow on the same tree; that the selfish seek happiness and do not find it, but find only Dead Sea fruit, while the unselfish dedicate themselves in self-forgetting service to others, and happiness comes to them, abundantly, and of itself. If now and then, we suffer temporary defeat, let us see that such defeat becomes a spur to stimulate to fresh endeavor, and not a stiletto to stab out high purpose. Let us thoughtfully remember that no life can be complete without suffering; that no culture can be mature, without sacrificial discipline; and that no love can reach its highest expression, until it is voiced in self-giving for the good of others.

Whatever may be our changeful experiences, through all the swirl of the restless, upheaving conditions about us, may we ever go bravely on, with spirits unbeaten, and with a conquering song within our hearts. Let us remember that just as the wondrous secrets of astronomy would not be disclosed, if it were always daylight, so also the deepest elements in human nature do not emerge and declare themselves, except in the nightfall of trial and emergency. Let us unwaveringly summon ourselves to endure our trials patiently, to fight our battles bravely, and forever to hold our integrity inviolably sacred, ever remembering that no good deed was ever lost, and that no worthy motive was ever penalized. And as birds forsake the wintry North and fly to the balmy South, singing through all their flight, so may we journey on to the Eternal Homeland, singing all the way thither. And when we come to the end of the day, with our work well done, may our Divine Savior conduct us to the Father's House of Many Mansions, where service and knowledge and fellowship and life shall be perfect forever.

Christmas 1930—New Year 1931

Reflection 22

With the returning of the Christmas and New Year
Season, when renewed emphasis is given to friendships both old and new, let me have the pleasure of sending
you the friendly and time-honored Wish: "A Merry Christmas and a Happy New Year." May you and all yours be given
the highest satisfactions of this Good Will Season, and may
such satisfactions abide with you and be multiplied unto
you, through all the unfolding future.

At this Anniversary Season, may we resolutely summon ourselves so to number our days that we may apply
our hearts unto wisdom,[44] and may we bring the Gold of
homage, the Frankincense of love, the Myrrh of sacrifice,
with unreserved dedication, to all the duties and relations
of life, ever remembering that the most valuable gift is not
the one that costs the most money, but the one that embodies the most good will and the highest fidelity.[45] May we be
unwaveringly constrained to measure every privilege and
duty, not by our comforts or our preferences, but by the
needs of humanity and the will of God.

As we look both backward and forward, may we be worthily grateful for the marvelous breath of life; for the wondrous
power of thought; for the priceless blessings of home; for the
dear memories of vanished faces whose smiles and love abide
ever with us; for the constant inspiration of understanding

friends; for the lofty privilege of work, and for the high spirit that appraises work as both dignified and ennobling; for the noble heritage that comes to us from the past; for every token of growing compassion toward needless suffering, anywhere and everywhere; and for every creative influence and agency for better cooperation in the matchless work of uplifting all mankind, both for today and tomorrow.

May we wisely recognize that unusually weighty problems are now confronting our country and all the world; and that multitudes are now experiencing privations and restrictions which lay a heavy toll, both upon the individual and the home. As never before, may we now faithfully recognize that those who are strong are inviolably bound to bear the burdens of the weak; that the spirit of altruistic cooperation should be enthroned throughout all organized society; that no conditions should be willingly tolerated which create an underprivileged class, or exploit any group for the advantage of another, or that magnify profit-seeking above the highest motive of service. May we hasten to give our best help to needy children; to lighten the burdens of the aged; to give practical sympathy to the poor; to voice our most helpful words and cooperation to the anxious victims of unemployment; to carry good cheer to the sick and lonely and discouraged—and thus may we help today and through all coming days. Whatever our difficulties and discouragements, may we go bravely on, remembering that life's highest progress has always been most surely registered, when circumstances have been most baffling, and when strength and fortitude have been put to the severest tests.

If unusual and most stressful tests have come or shall come to us, in life's practical affairs, may we be given the invincible spirit of our brave forebears, who revealed the splendor of their souls when days were dark and difficult. Let us not ask for tasks equal to our strength, but for strength equal to our tasks, that we may know the daily miracle of doing the impossible. Let us thoughtfully remember that God's plan for us is not to lessen our duties, but to enlarge our privileges; not to decrease our burdens, but to increase our strength. In all our battles and burdens, may we trustfully look to Him Who came to give the Life More Abundant. May we remember that no life is nobly complete that has not suffered; no culture is richly mature that is not the result of severe discipline and real self-sacrifice; no love is worthy of Him Who went about doing good, unless such love shall be voiced in self-giving for the sake of others.

By the brevity of the earthly life and its measureless possibilities, may we be unceasingly challenged to live for objectives that are of supreme importance, and not for tawdry things that perish with the passing day. May we steadfastly refuse to allow any room in our lives for petty and ignoble ambitions; for secret vindictiveness and blind prejudice; for narrow bigotry and unreasoned intolerance; for shams and insincerities; for grouchiness, pessimism, cynicism, uncharitableness, and all sharp-thorned discontent—remembering wisely that all such maladies of mind and heart discolor and disfigure the whole landscape of life. May we always be given the poise and power of fairmindedness; a dominant sense of the supremacy and eternity of righteousness; an uncompromising warfare against all wrong standards and conditions; and an unhesitating willingness to make any and every needed sacrifice for the public trust and the common good.

If we must sometimes be called to travel some lonely road far into the sullen night; if we must feel the dull ache of some hurt of yesterday, or must walk in the hush of some trying ordeal, today or tomorrow; if we must sometimes be misunderstood, and eat the bread of sorrow,[46] and dwell in the House of Pain—may we be given the Faith that can triumphantly go alone in the dark, the Love that suffereth long and is kind, the Hope that grows brighter and stronger unto the Perfect Day. If we have relaxed our hold on the higher things, may we at once resolve, with help Divine, henceforth to walk in the Better Way, until the Sunset Lights shall close the earthly day. And then, may we be given an abundant entrance into the "Glad homeland, not far away, where none are sick, or poor, or lone, the place where we shall find our own"[47]—the Eternal Home prepared by Him Who brought Life and Immortality to Light through His Gospel, and Who has given His own guarantee of the eternal blessedness of all who are willing to be His friends.

Christmas 1931—New Year 1932

Reflection 23

From my Study, where it is my ever-increasing delight to have fellowship with all ages and conditions of our busy, battling, burdened humanity, let me send to you and yours, the age-old but ever-perennial greeting: "A Merry Christmas and a Prosperous New Year." And this greeting is meant not only for this current Christmas and New Year Season, with its haunting charms, its wistful memories, its beckoning hopes, its renewed opportunity for the expression of friendliness and good will, but also, for all the unfolding and unending future.

As our hearts thrill again with the zest and tang of the Christmas Spirit, may we now hear more clearly than ever before, the prophetic Song of the Angelic Choir at Bethlehem: "Glory to God in the highest, and on earth Peace, Good Will toward men." May we summon ourselves anew, in the midst of all the clamor and confusion of our perplexed and troubled world, to dedicate our utmost strength, to further the cause of Peace and Good Will, everywhere, and always. May we envisage a world wherein the golden rule of mutual responsibility and good will shall one day become triumphant through all the earth.

At this Season for accentuated emphasis upon home reunions, and upon friendships both old and new, let us worthily relight the candles of good cheer and cooperative helpfulness, for those who are experiencing privations and restrictions which lay a heavy toll upon their homes and hearts. May we so voice our understanding sympathy and good will, as to give them new heart and hope, for all the days and duties ahead. Let us especially voice our best cheer for the little children and the aged; for the orphan and the underprivileged; for the poor and the needy; for the afflicted and the unfortunate; for the lonely and the discouraged; for the derelict and the unfriended. May we be experts in doing good to all, and in giving hurt to none.

As we pass from the Old Year to the New, let us make a faithful inventory of all the higher values of life, even as we make such inventory of life's temporal affairs. Let us leave to the past all lingering asperities and bitter memories; all ugly jealousies and ungenerous competitions; all unreasoning prejudices and uncharitable judgments. Let us discard all worthless luggage, and repledge our highest and best to the supreme things, as we face the unknown days and demands awaiting us. May we faithfully realize that our Divinely appointed mission in the earthly life is to do more than to make a living—we are to make a life. Let us not spoil the one, in seeking to gain the other. When we are tempted to take the short look, and allow ourselves to become self-centered place-seekers, may we quickly hear the Great Master's pained rebuke: "Whosoever would be first among you, shall be servant of all."[48] May our lives be so rich in gracious words and deeds, that no loss of money or of health can ever make us poor.

Despite the murky bewilderment of the momentous and fast-changing days through which we are passing, let us go forward with purposes more thoughtfully intrepid, and with faith more sacrificially adventurous than ever before. May we be enabled to think clearly and without self-deception; to speak without pretense or exaggeration; to eschew utterly every subtle device of indirection and insincerity; and to act always with straightforward integrity. May we be given the wisdom and strength and courage, in scorn of consequence, inflexibly to devote our lives to the things worth living for, and if need be, worth dying for. In this critically testing hour for ourselves, for our country, and for the whole world, let us look wisely to our ideals and standards, remembering that high above all other standards is the standard of righteousness. May we vitally realize that our lives and our institutions are built upon the sand, if they are not built upon righteousness;[49] and may our consciences be ever-increasingly intoned to a far higher devotion to righteousness, in all the realms of life-personal, domestic, social, financial, governmental, educational, moral and religious. Ever and forever, may we devote our worthiest thought and service to build all life upon the sure foundations of righteousness, knowing well that both the being and the well-being of civilized, orderly and enduring society must rest upon such foundations.

Realizing that we are so bound together in the bundle of life, that the hurt of one is the concern of all, and that the welfare of all should be the concern of each, may we worthily know that it is not enough to rescue some injured traveler on life's Jericho road, but we are also inviolably bound to make the road safe for every traveler.[50] Let us ever be mindful that no one shall fall under a burden which may be lifted by us. May we face all life's duties, as seeing Him Who is invisible. May we know that His way is the only safe and satisfying way, for the individual and the home; for capital and for labor; for the church and for the state; for all the

realms of life. Above all the plaintive voices of depression
and discouragement, of broken plans and shattered expec-
tations, of cynical unfaith and unreckoning disobedience,
there comes the one clear call from the Throne of Eternal
Righteousness: "This is the way—walk ye in it."[51] In Him
alone may we find the total and final meaning of life.

As we journey on, may we learn to walk as blithely in
the deep chasms where no sun shines, as upon the lighted
mountain tops; and to maintain brave hearts in the midst of
life's storms, as well as in its calms. If we would fain evade
difficulties, hardships, sufferings and tears, may we remember that as the untempered steel is of little service, so is the
untempered life. May we know that it takes more than sunshine and laughter to produce the strongest and most useful
lives—the cloud and the rainfall and sometimes the storm
must also play their part. Whatever the testing emergency
that may come to us—the heavy burden; the harsh discouragement in life's temporal affairs; the smiting wind of disappointment; the invasion of death into the inner circle of
our lives—whatever our Valley of Achor[52] may be—may we
be ever unafraid and triumphant, because of our anchorage
to Him Who is there within the shadows, keeping watch
above His own. May we know the glory of bravely going on,
when life's road seems steep and its burden heavy, remembering that the struggler may sometimes wearily give up
when in sight of the golden crown. In all the experiences
of the earthly journey, whether amid scenes of mingled joy
and pain, or under clouds wrapped in beauty and lined with
golden glow, may the Immortal Hope unceasingly beckon
us, onward and upward, until we go to the Father's House
and greet again our absent loved ones who have vanished

from us, through the passing years. And with Him and with them, in the Forever Land, may we journey on in the perfect fulfillment of the infinitely blessed destiny which He has purposed for His friends.

Christmas 1932—New Year 1933

Reflection 24

As we come again to the Mid-Year Holiday Season, when the world is echoing the remindful greetings, "Merry Christmas" and "Happy New Year," let me send you this friendly card, voicing my cordial salutations and prayerful good wishes for you and yours, for this gladful Season, and through all the days ahead.

This Annual Season is proverbially the time when we are freshly challenged to survey life's friendships, old and new, and to see that our friendships are kept in worthy repair, faithfully remembering the Biblical injunction: "Thine own friend, and thy father's friend, forsake not."[53] May the highest meanings of the joyful Christmastide and of the beckoning New Year enter abidingly into our lives, and be translated into the love that manifests itself in unceasing good will toward all mankind, and into the joy that rings Christmas bells the whole year round.

At this Anniversary Season, when both Memory and Hope are given added emphasis, may the quickened remembrance of our gracious and countless blessings evoke our profoundest gratitude—for our dear home loves, with their sacred loyalties; for faithful friends, with their ever-inspiring friendliness; for the glorious heritage bequeathed us from noble forebears; for the high discipline of life's daily work and burdens; for every Wayside Spring that blesses us on life's journey; and above all, for Him whose coming gave a new conception to all the relationships of life.

As the Wise Men of old followed the Star to Him who came at the first Christmas, so may we follow Him whom they sought, wherever He shall lead.[54] May we dedicate all our powers to help all humankind, as He helped them—the eager young people, with their unfolding responsibilities; the aged, whose burdens should ever be worthily shared by those who are younger; the workers in life's midday years, who are heavily weighted with battles and burdens; the poor and needy, the suffering and afflicted, the wronged and oppressed, the unfriended and the outcast—even all who wear our human life, whatever their race, creed, country, or condition.

As we pass from the Old Year through the swinging gates of the New, may we be steadfastly resolved "So to number our days that we may apply our hearts unto wisdom."[55] May we turn from the past, with its futile regrets to follow revitalized purposes to noblest goals in the veiled future. May we wisely realize that it matters little what kind of a house one lives in, but it matters much what kind of a person lives in the house. May we put far from us the world's tawdry prizes, the lust of display, and the vanity of cheap applause. May we be kept from all pettiness and littleness, all cynicism and embitterment, all hurtful prejudice and unthinking intolerance, all rancor and ill-will—from all those maladies of mind and moods of spirit that would despoil life of its highest worth. And may our lives be dominated by the love that envieth not, vaunteth not itself, seeketh not her own, rejoiceth in the truth, never faileth.[56]

In these momentous days, when our country and the whole world are being tested by abnormal and swift-changing conditions—may we be given wisdom and help above ourselves, and a faith which sees beyond the murky confusion of today to the coming of a better tomorrow. May our consciences be so acutely quickened that we shall feel deeply the sin and shame of selfish war, and private greed, and social injustice, and whatever else alienates life from life, class from class, and nation from nation. May we ever link our lives with humanity-lifting causes, fronting always toward the light and toward the right. May our every talent be dedicated for the bringing in of that halcyon day when righteousness and justice and fidelity and love may so unite mankind that the strength of the race shall be expended in going forward and upward to the heights of a redeemed and righteous world.

Let us bravely journey on in the triumphant confidence that the best is yet to come. May the veiled providences that are bound up with our lives disclose to us glorious surprises, at every step of our untraveled future. May we read the trials of life, not as accidents of earth, but as a Divine discipline for our larger happiness and usefulness. May we pass through all these trials unembittered, attuned to deeper sympathy with others, ennobled in character, and strengthened in faith. May we increasingly know that our confidence is not in some dark, impersonal Fate, but in One Who is infinite in wisdom and power and love, and Who sets all human life in the light of Immortality. And when our day's work is done, may there be light for us at the Eventide, and then, a bridge of Sunset for us to the Morning Land where our Lord has prepared an Eternal Home for all who will follow Him. May He graciously receive us unto that Home, where with Him we shall perfectly know and do His will, in an unshadowed reunion which shall last forever.

Christmas 1933—New Year 1934

Reflection 25

The joyful music of the returning Christmas and New Year Season echoes again throughout the earth, and all mankind is challenged afresh by the conquering notes of the old-time, Angel Symphony: "Glory to God in the highest, and on earth peace, good will toward men." At this festal Season of reunited home gatherings, and of added and deepened friendships, let me voice for you and yours, the full measure of friendliness and good will that is voiced by the age-old salutations: "A Merry Christmas," and "A Happy New Year."

Deeply suggestive is the saying: "God gave us memory that we might have roses in December."[57] If memory is to bring us roses in December, we must learn what to forget, as well as what to remember. We must learn how wisely to forget our blunders, losses, injuries, sorrows, successes, and, most of all, through His grace, to forget our sins. Likewise, we are now summoned anew to take faithful account of life's highest values and blessings. Memory constrains us to voice our deepest gratitude for our gracious heritage of blessings—for the priceless blessings of our homes; for friendships old and new; for days of challenge and struggle; for the privilege and glory of work; for sorrows that come to refine us, and to make us more helpful to others; for the golden dream that selfish war will one day be finally hushed throughout all the earth, and all mankind shall keep step by the law of love; and, above all, for Him Who touches all life into highest meaning, both for today and for the unending tomorrow.

At this beckoning Season, may the gentleness of the Prince of Peace touch us to a more considerate helpfulness for all humanity—for little children and for the lonely aged; for the poor and needy and underprivileged and discouraged; for those who keep punctual tryst with grief and wakeful vigil with pain; for those whose faith falters in the midst of mysterious providences; for those who watch with wearied eyes for ships that do not arrive; and for those whose cheeks are flushed with victory, let us not fail to pray that they may be given the grace to carry the full cup of their prosperity, with becoming humility. Through all seasons, may we be experts in helping all mankind, remembering that in due season, the bread of kindness cast upon the waters of human need, will return after many days, with a wonderful increase.[58]

In this hour of the world's pathetic bewilderment and baffling problems, may we listen more alertly than ever before, to the supreme message that was heralded by the angels; and may we henceforth strive with our utmost power, to incarnate this message, in universal human relations. While many voices may be heard, in these perplexing days, proclaiming their various panaceas for the world's ills, may we go on with the profound and ever-deepening conviction that there is no complete and abiding solution to be expected of the world's problems, whether personal, social, racial, economic, political, national, international, moral or religious, save as we are faithful to the teaching of the Prince of Peace, and are ready to fulfill all the requirements of sacrificial love. May we increasingly realize that the whole world is now one vast neighborhood; that neither nations nor individuals can live to themselves; that pagan ideals and methods cannot save our civilization; that a persistent, pagan civilization will perish as completely as the fabled Atlantis;[59] and that if our civilization is to be saved, it must be saved and dominated by Him, about Whom the angels sang on the first Christmas morning.

As we journey on, may we be given an ever-enlarging reverence for the sacredness and the indefeasible rights of every human life. May we turn from all broken cisterns wherein there is no water, to Him Who is the Living Water, and within the sanctuary of Whose Heart there is ever an adequate shelter for all baffled minds and burdened hearts.[60] May we go on in the confident faith that He has a gracious purpose for our little lives, and that He will bring such purpose to a glorious fruition, if we will follow where He leads. Let us evermore dare to live for the supreme things of life, faithfully remembering that in the long last, nothing counts but character, integrity, love, sacrifice, service. If life's trail shall sometimes take us into the night, may we know that it is better to walk with Him in the dark, than to walk alone in the light. Anchored to Him, may we go bravely on, triumphant in the faith that the trail of our mortal years runs out at the threshold of the House of Many Mansions. And when the trail dips down into the Valley of Shadows, may we fear no evil,[61] because He shall company with us, our Redeemer, our Pilot, our Companion forever.

Christmas 1934—New Year 1935

Reflection 26[62]

CHRISTMAS MESSAGE FROM PASTOR

Cable from Port Said, Egypt
December 18, 1935
Robert H. Coleman[63]
Dallas, Texas

Our best love for our dear church and our best wishes for everybody in homeland for Christmas and beyond always.

GEORGE W. TRUETT

Reflection 27

In the deepest and most inward sense, let me voice for you all the age-old greeting: "A Merry Christmas and A Happy New Year!" May this returning Good-Will Season be a season of growing love and peace and power, sustained by the living Spirit of our Lord Jesus Christ!

Surely, our hearts are filled with deep joy and gratitude to God, as we recall the growing evidences of Christian faith and zeal that crowd upon us, as we survey religious conditions around the encircling globe. New chapters of the Acts of the Apostles are being written in the Far East. In India and Burma, China and Japan, the word of the Cross[64] has won multitudes whose loyalty, self-sacrifice, courage, and consecrated gifts are an earnest of larger conquests to be won. Our Lord has mightily acknowledged the witness of our Baptist people in the Orient, in Africa, in South America, in Continental Europe, and throughout sixty-nine nations of the earth. Vast are the opportunities open to us, if we abide in Him, "Without Whom we can do nothing."[65] Nor would we withhold thankful praise for all we have seen and heard of evangelical advance made by our fellow Christians of every name. We would fervently say with Paul: "Grace be with all them that love our Lord Jesus Christ in sincerity."[66]

We are facing times of stern testing. Avowed atheism has become aggressive, and in some lands religion is assailed as "dope."[67] As Christians and citizens, we must seek to confound such assaults by the quality of our life and service. "Let your light so shine before men that they may see your good works and glorify your Father who is in heaven."[68]

Materialism abounds, and its subtle taint appears even in the churches of Jesus Christ. It can be met only by the sacrificial spirit of Him who taught that "A man's life consisteth not in the abundance of the things that he possesseth."[69]

Christian moral standards, and even elementary decencies, are ridiculed; they can be vindicated only by the holy life which carries the evidence of its own worth, and through which the Holy Spirit "will convince the world of sin."[70]

The peril of war is grave, and it is for the servants of the Prince of Peace to pray and labor for the removal of the political and social and economic causes of ill-will, and above all for the winning of men and women the world over to Him, the fruit of whose Spirit is peace.[71]

Religious liberty is imperiled in widely scattered regions of the earth, and we are thankful that our Baptist World Alliance has, again and again, by its intervention, enlarged freedom in some lands, and preserved it in others. But we must be prepared to meet a serious and growing menace to the doctrine which is among the most distinctive and precious elements of our Baptist heritage.

"He must reign till He hath put all enemies under His Feet."[72] There is the firm foundation of our confidence. Rooted and grounded in Him,[73] let us all—the millions who are banded together in the Baptist faith and order, together with all other friends of Christ—resolve to confront the multiple challenges of our time with a renewed and deepened consecration. We must pray more earnestly: we have not exhausted the "unsearchable riches of God."[74] Must we not believe that He who, in the course of a century, has multiplied our numbers twenty-three times over, making the Baptist communion the largest Free Church fellowship on earth, wills that the churches He has called into being shall play a worthy part in the extension of His Kingdom? The opportunities are boundless; may 1937 find us by His grace faithful to our high calling!

Christmas 1936—New Year 1937

Reflection 28

With the returning Christmas and New Year Season, let me greet you in the name of our Lord Jesus Christ, and voice every best wish for you, for the Happy Holiday Season, and beyond, always!

As we come again, through God's gracious mercy, to this happy Season, may all our hearts be humble, grateful and joyful, and may we fervently pray with Tiny Tim: "God bless us every one!"[75]

By the goodness and mercy wherewith He crowns our lives, let us be wholeheartedly constrained, both to pray and to labor, without ceasing, for the happiness and betterment of the poor and the needy and the neglected; for precious children who are in any way handicapped; for those who have scarcely known a mother's love, or a father's care; for underprivileged and overburdened men and women; for all who are lonely and bereaved and disappointed; for those whose lives are severely tested by strange and fiery trials; for the meanest and basest and lowest of our fellow humanity; and for all our bludgeoned and fear-ridden world.

These are days of fierce challenge. In wide areas of the earth, religious liberty has been ruthlessly trampled underfoot, and in others, it is gravely menaced. Vast areas throughout the earth are distraught by oppressive injustices, by stupid hates, and by ghastly wars. Such days need us, at our highest and best, both in thought and in service. Let those of us who enjoy complete freedom of worship, thank God afresh for this priceless privilege, and let us faithfully remember that such a treasure is retained only by ceaseless vigilance. Irreligion is widespread. Questions of finance and trade, of treaties and covenants, of diplomacy and legislation, and other similar problems have their large and rightful place in our thoughts; but, fundamentally, the paramount and indispensable need of mankind lies not in economic or political adjustments, very important as these are, but in true penitence for our wrong living, and in trustful faith and submissive obedience to our Divine Savior and Lord. Let us turn ever to Him Who loves unto the uttermost, and Who has chosen to be influenced by our humble and submissive prayers.

As we journey on, may we ever be given the watchful eye, the considerate heart, and the unselfish hand, to the end that we may ever-increasingly walk in the steps of Him Who went about doing good. Let us steadfastly refuse to allow the grilling trials of the world so to overcome us that we shall forget its glorious benedictions. To the utmost, and to the last, let us live to make permanent and regnant throughout all the earth, the song of the angels: "Glory to God in the highest, and on earth, peace, good will toward men."

Christmas 1937—New Year 1938

Reflection 29

As we stand at the portals of another Christmas and New Year Season, when the Carols of Joy and Peace and Good Will fill all the air, let me most earnestly voice for you and yours the prayerful wish that the larger meaning of the age-old Christmas Carols may be more deeply written in our own and all other lives today, and through all the days to come. Let us sing with Whittier:

> Blow bugles of battle, the marches of peace;
> East, West, North and South, let the long quarrel cease;
> Sing the song of Great Joy that the angels began,
> Sing the Glory of God, and of Good Will to Man.[76]

At this happy season when we have the double joy of remembering and of being remembered, may we be doubly inspired with visions of service, wide as the needs of mankind and broad as the love of God. May we worthily remember the poor, the friendless, the underprivileged, the overburdened, the unfortunate, the afflicted in body and in mind, the lonely and discouraged in spirit, ever remembering to voice our most Christlike compassion for all who sin and suffer and sorrow, around the encircling globe.

It is written with fiery emphasis, the whole world over, that we have reached the incomparably fateful time when stupendous forces and influences are shaking the world to its very foundations.[77] Surely we should all now wisely remember that unless all life shall be built on the granite foundations of righteousness, it will be built on the sinking sand. The deadly menace of materialism casts its baleful shadow in all realms and among all peoples. The astounding fact of persecution, racial and religious, continues to challenge the world with horror, and to make a blot that is an unspeakable disgrace to civilization. Fear seems to have the pass-key to whole nations, as well as to myriads of individuals, whether in palace or in cottage. Vast changes are rapidly sweeping the world, as swirling ocean currents sweep the seas. These changes are economic and financial, governmental and political, educational and social, moral and religious. The world is still in the dreadful aftermath of the most ghastly and widely desolating war in the history of mankind.[78] The instability of reconstruction continues to vex the nations, both large and small. Misunderstandings, national and international, seem relentless in their persistence. The revival of the philosophies of terror and hate, in various sections of the earth; the clash of classes in all lands; overwrought nerves in a high-powered world—all these conditions remind us how desperately we need help above ourselves.

On every hand the searching question emerges: Is there an adequate remedy for the poignantly troubled world situation of today? Is there a door of hope in the Valley of Achor? Is there any physician, anywhere, who is able to heal the awful hurts of our wounded humanity? Does our sinning, suffering humanity have a Helper anywhere, who is able to sound the awful depths of our manifold needs? With unfaltering conviction, the glorious Christmas Story gives its positive answer to the crucial question. "And the angel said unto them, Fear not: for, behold I bring you good tidings of great joy, which shall be to all people. For unto you is born this day in the city of David, a Savior, Who is Christ the Lord."[79] The ancient prophet had foretold His coming in these vivid words: "For unto us a child is born, unto us a Son is given: and the government shall be upon His shoulder: and His name shall be called Wonderful, Counsellor, the Mighty God, the Everlasting Father, the Prince of Peace."[80]

What a happy, beautiful, wonderful world shall this world be, when our needy humanity will faithfully walk in the ways of our infinitely gracious Savior and Lord! He is the one all-sufficient mediator between God and man,[81] between man and man, and between nation and nation. He is the Mighty Daysman, the Great Reconciler. When men really love Him, they will also love one another. He is the outstanding miracle of all the ages. The searchlight of criticism has been focused upon Him, both by friends and by foes, for the long, long centuries, and yet it has failed to find in Him one suggestion of sin, one ill-advised word, one selfish deed. He was born in the first century, yet He belongs to all the centuries. He was born a Jew, yet He belongs to all races. He was born in Bethlehem, yet He belongs to all countries. His challenging call is alike to Saxon, or Teuton, or Mongolian, or Slav, or Latin, to come penitently to Him for His forgiving grace and His empowering help. Oh! Who would not wish to follow in His train, in all the swift-changing years of time, and throughout the ceaseless cycles of eternity?

Christmas 1938—New Year 1939

Reflection 30

At this recurring Christmas and New Year Season, when happy home reunions are had, and when tokens of Friendship and Good Will are sent from friends to friends, I would send you a gift, not of silver and gold, but a gift of the heart, voiced in the fervently prayerful wish for your highest happiness and usefulness, for this joyful Season—and, beyond, for all the unfolding and unending tomorrows!

Charles Dickens rightly saw in the Christmas Season a renewed challenge to us all, to voice our best greetings, not only to family and friends, but, also, to voice our vitally sympathetic interest in all classes and conditions of humanity. Especially, should our practical sympathy be voiced for the poor and needy, the underprivileged and unfortunate, the aged and infirm, the bereaved and sorrowing, the prodigal and the derelict. And such cooperative sympathy should be voiced, not only during the Holiday Season, but through all seasons, and for all peoples, everywhere. The world is filled with lives in poignant need of understanding and practical sympathy, and one language can be understood by everybody, and that is the language of good will and unselfish helpfulness. "Love never faileth!"[82]

The real meaning of the Christmas Season is given in the announcement of the Angel to the Shepherds: "Fear not; for, behold, I bring you good tidings of great joy, which shall be to all people. For unto you is born this day, in the City of David, a Savior, who is Christ the Lord."[83] And, then, a multitude of the heavenly host echoed the glorious refrain: "Glory to God in the highest, and on earth, Peace, Good Will toward men."[84] This is the supreme message for our sorely troubled world today—a world in which fear and war and tyranny and injustice and suffering and death are in awful evidence, throughout vast sections of earth. How harshly the Bethlehem Chorus seems out of tune, with the awful realities in the world today! Pagan gods of selfish greed and cruel hate have turned much of the world into blood-soaked shambles, and through all sorts of propaganda, are seeking to paganize the whole world. Wars and rumors of wars, international bad faith, broken peace pacts, intolerance, injustice, cruelty, and sordid manifestations of self-seeking and stupidity are in evidence, on such a vast scale as to be a worldwide menace to civilization.

In these incomparably fateful days, God speaks to us the stabilizing exhortation to which we should all give constant and faithful heed: "Be still, and know that I am God."[85] The supremely determining factor in the world's future is God. And so, today, notwithstanding wars, and gravely distressful situations, on a world scale, Jesus is God's Ambassador of Good Will to all mankind; and He comes with Heaven's overtures of peace, for "God was in Christ reconciling the world unto Himself."[86] His Peace is higher and deeper than any and all worldly circumstances. The conflicts of life, however fierce and disturbing, are incidental and passing, but the Peace of God which passeth all understanding is fundamental and abiding.[87] All the world's Herods shall perish,[88] but Jesus is eternal. Vastly significant are the words of Napoleon to one of his officers: "The Spirit of Christ overcomes me. Caesar and Alexander and myself have founded Empires, but we rested the creation of our genius on force. Jesus has founded an Empire on Love; and at this hour, millions would die for Him."[89] His words, His works, His character are altogether sufficient to attest Him as the one only adequate Savior for all mankind. Our supreme need is to know Him as the Strength of our lives, the Inspiration of our thinking, the Director of our conduct, the Hope of our souls. Since God, our gracious Heavenly Father, gives His only begotten Son for us, let us be utterly unwilling to give Him less than our best.

It is always midnight somewhere in the world. Even so, as it is written on a famous sundial in England: "It is always morning somewhere in the world." That is the word for us today, and all the days. As we look at vast sections of our world today, they are as unpromising as darkness, and as ominous as the grave. Violence and tyranny seem to be invincible. Sin and moral chaos appear to rule with unrelenting fury. Just as surely, however, there are vast sections of our world today which are full of promise, and radiant with hopeful outlook. These are the morning places, where the sun is shining, and the denizens of darkness are being driven to their lairs. God is on His throne, and all rebellion against Him must go down before His Divine purpose and power. It is always morning somewhere, and by and by it is going to be morning everywhere. "He must reign till He hath put all His enemies under His feet."[90] One day, war will be under His feet forever—may God hasten that glorious day! The days of sin and selfishness and suffering cannot always last. "Weeping may endure for a night, but joy cometh in 'the morning.'"[91] One day, death shall be under His feet, so that even the very prospect calls forth the triumphant shout: "Thanks be unto God, who giveth us the victory through our Lord Jesus Christ."[92]

Let us be done, once and for all, with the spirit of unfaith and defeatism and fear. With all-conquering courage and faith, let us, as we close the gates of the Old Year, and enter the portals of the New Year, rededicate our all to build all life, personal, social, business, professional, national, international, moral and religious, on the eternal foundations of righteousness and love. Let us say with Thorwaldsen,[93] who, when asked what was his greatest statue, promptly replied: "The next one." With Kipling, let us resolutely say: "We can make good all loss, except the loss of turning back."[94] And say with Dan Crawford: "Hats off to the past, coats off to the future."[95] And say with Rupert Brooke: "Now God be thanked who matched us with this hour."[96] May He lift us above all pettiness and self-seeking, all false ambitions and misspent endeavors; and may He constrainingly center all our purposes in His blessed will, ever inspiring us wisely to remember that the highest duty and privilege of life is to do His will. More and more, may we realize how great and good a thing is life, when it is lived in the reverent fear of God, and in wholehearted devotion to that which He approves.

As we sometimes peer through the Westward Windows, and think of our passage through the Sunset Gate, let us unfearingly trust ourselves to Him Who guides the birds in their long and uncharted migrations, and Whose purpose in coming to earth, in the first Christmas, long ago, was to be the Way and Truth and Life and Light and Love for all our needy world! Thus following Him, we shall arrive at the Morning Gate, in His own good time, to live forever with Him, and with all who are willing to be His friends.

Christmas 1939—New Year 1940

Reflection 34

As we come again to the happy Christmas and New Year Season, let this modest greeting bear to you and yours my most cordial good wishes, both for the present, and for all the untraveled future.

At this supreme Season of the year, for joyful family reunions, and for the renewal and deepening of life's inspiring friendships, let us seek to make the Season still more joyous, by helpful ministries to the poor and needy, to the aged and lonely, to the bereaved and suffering, remembering the hauntingly blessed words: "Inasmuch as ye did it unto one of the least of these My brethren, ye did it unto Me."[97]

This wistful Season is one when both Memory and Hope stir deeply in the heart. James Barrie tells us that "God gave us memory that we might have roses in December."[98] If memory is to bring only roses in December, we must learn what to forget, as well as what to remember. Life is too brief, and great, and responsible, to be wasted on futile regrets. Charles Lamb says that the person is either very bad or very ignorant, who does not make a good resolution on New Year's Day.[99] To make new mistakes is human; to repeat old ones is stupid. "Forgetting the things which are behind, and stretching forward to the things which are before,"[100] we are, as did Paul, to let the memories of yesterday and the visions of tomorrow, challenge us to be faithful to the Divinely appointed meaning and mission of our lives.

In one of his charming essays, Robert Louis Stevenson says that "A happy man or woman is a better thing to find than a five-pound note. Their entrance into a room is as though another candle had been lighted."[101] In these tremendous and anxious days, ours is a tempered joy. Every thoughtful person must be poignantly aware that the present world situation is one of the gravest in all human history. Two philosophies of life, Individualism and Totalitarianism, are in a death grapple. The world is now witnessing an outbreak of barbarism which is a menace to the whole earth. All the ethical standards of the world are distinctly challenged by present world conditions. Ruthless bombs over beautiful and historic cities, and over helpless men, women and little children; poisonous hatreds, economic pressure, hunger, starvation, and destruction send out their darkening shadows throughout the whole earth. But, unspeakably terrible as is the situation, it is not a hopeless situation, because of God. Ceaselessly we are to sing with the Psalmist: "The Lord God omnipotent reigneth."[102] And though clouds and darkness are round about Him, yet righteousness and justice are the foundation of His throne.[103] Evil is not to have a permanent triumph in this world. It may win momentary success, but it is inexorably doomed, because of the eternally triumphant truth voiced by Lowell: "Standeth God within the shadows, keeping watch above His own."[104]

For long years, the two South American Republics of Argentina and Chile disputed and warred over the location of a boundary. Finally, the two countries erected a towering statue of Christ, on a peak of the Andes Mountains, three miles above the ocean, upon a boundary line between the two countries. Upon the pedestal of the statue were carved these great words: "The mountains will crumble to dust ere Argentines and Chileans break the peace which, at the feet of Christ the Redeemer; they have sworn to keep."[105] May the Peace-bringing Christ Who is typified in that statue on the Andes, soon bring a righteous and abiding peace to all our war-torn world. Looking beyond the wild confusion of this hour, with its wide region of cruelty and terror and suffering, let us wisely and unceasingly labor to make perpetual and universal, the song of the angels over the cradle at Bethlehem: "Glory to God in the highest, and on earth peace, good will toward men."

We are to face the unknown New Year unafraid, because God lives and loves and reigns. Longfellow thus voices our faith for us:

> And in despair I bowed my head;
> "There is no peace on Earth," I said;
> "For hate is strong, and mocks the song
> Of peace on earth, good will to men."
>
> Then pealed the bells more loud and deep;
> "God is not dead, nor doth He sleep!
> The wrong shall fail, the right prevail.
> With peace on earth, good will to men."[106]

As we face the future, let us be utterly unwilling to insulate ourselves and to ignore the vital problems of our own land and of all other lands. No sections of the world are detached and isolated, but all are interdependent and bound together by our mechanized, high-powered, and fast-moving civilization. Let us see faithfully to our standards of character and conduct, realizing that false standards and pagan ideas could be more destructive than would be an unarmed invasion. The uncompromising attitude of the immortal Washington is to be ours, when right is involved: "Let us raise a standard to which the wise and just may repair; the result is in the hands of God."[107] And the late President Wilson said in his last message to the world: "Our civilization cannot survive materially, unless it be redeemed Spiritually. It can be saved only by being permeated with the Spirit of Christ, and by being made free and happy by the practices which spring out of that Spirit."[108] In our beloved land, where free peoples joyfully live together in mutual cooperation, may there now be a rededication on all fronts, to the nobly historic and righteous landmarks, bequeathed to us by our heroic forebears, and for which they were willing both to live and to die. With a great price they obtained the great liberties that now are ours—the liberty of thought and of speech, the liberty of public assembly, and of religious worship.

The death knell of these priceless liberties has been sounded over large sections of the earth, by vast and unrelenting totalitarian systems. This standard must be maintained, whatever the cost: "God alone is Lord of the conscience." The early founders and builders believed in God—the God of eternal righteousness and love, and they faithfully proclaimed that obedience to His will should be the supreme law of our lives. In that glorious faith, let us joyfully and courageously face all the issues of today and of the coming tomorrow!

> Ring in the valiant man and free,
> The larger heart, the kindlier hand;
> Ring out the darkness of the land,
> Ring in the Christ that is to be.[109]

Christmas 1940—New Year 1941

Reflection 32

At this returning Christmas and New Year Season, when friends are challenged to be better friends, and strangers to become friends, let me send you and yours, the age-old Greeting: "A Merry Christmas and a Happy New Year."

This "Good Will" season returns to us, in one of the most ominous and momentous hours, in all human history. Never was our war-torn, troubled world more desperately in need of the Christmas Message, than it is today: "Fear not; for, behold, I bring you good tidings of great joy which shall be to all people. For unto you is born this day in the city of David, a Savior, Who is Christ the Lord." And again: "Glory to God in the Highest, and on earth peace, good will toward men."[110]

The Christmastide is preeminently the season for voicing gratitude and gladness, by renewed tokens of love and friendship, beginning with the home, and going out into all the relations of life. Especially is it the season when an understanding and practical sympathy is voiced for the poor and needy; for the little children and for the aged; for the afflicted and the underprivileged; for the bereaved, the unfortunate, the disappointed. An old Bible picture points the way for us: "They helped everyone his neighbor, and every one said to his brother, Be of good courage."[111] An old Persian proverb teaches us: "I complained because I had no shoes, until I saw a man who had no feet." A poet searches us with his questions:

> Did you give him a lift? He's a brother of man,
> And bearing about all the burden he can.
> Did you give him a word? He was downcast and blue,
> And the right kind of word might have helped him get
>   through.
> Did you stretch out your hand, and pass him a smile?
> It might have meant victory, that last weary mile.
> Did you do the right thing, and point out the road,
> Or did you just let him go by with his load?[112]

We are ever to remember that all worthy and abiding success in life is to be measured, not by what the world gives us, but by what we give the world.

In this incomparably fateful hour for humanity, everywhere, we must do more than read papers, and listen to radio commentators, who daily remind us of the unspeakable tragedies and sufferings of the whole world. The entire world is now at the crossroads, all its ethical standards are being brazenly challenged, and we are now facing one of the most ominous and momentous crises of all history. But, gravely critical and difficult as is the hour now facing America and all the world, it is not an hour for fear and defeatism and unfaith, but an hour for unwavering faith, and high-souled courage, and noblest behavior. Certainly, an indescribable horror chills our hearts as we think of war—bloody, merciless, inhuman war! But let us remember that there are some things more precious than life. The poet is right:

> Though love repine and reason chafe,
> There comes a voice without reply,
> 'Tis man's perdition to be safe,
> When for the truth he ought to die.[113]

Patriotism has ever been one of the loftiest passions of the human heart, from the day when the weeping captives sat down by the rivers of Babylon, and vowed to one another that they would never forget Jerusalem.[114] The heart must always be thrilled by the patriotic cry of young Rupert Brooke, of the first World War: "If I should die, think this of me, that there's some corner of a foreign field that is forever England."[115] Vast is the message on the Statue of Ben Hill, in Atlanta: "Who saves his country saves all things, and all things saved do bless him. Who lets his country die, lets all things die, dies himself ignobly, and all things dying, curse him." If government of the people, by the people, for the people, is to endure, then the great freedoms—of speech, of press, of religion—must be upheld, whatever the cost!

As we fervently sing: "God bless America," let us wisely remember that He is a God of righteousness, and that He has principles by which He governs both nations and individuals, which principles He cannot, and will not compromise. "Righteousness exalteth a nation, but sin is a reproach to any people."[116] The supreme question ever to ask is: "Is it right?" Principles do not change. There are moral principles and eternal values that must never be trifled with. An ancient prophet points the way for us—"To do justly, to love mercy, and to walk humbly with God."[117] Another prophet warns us: "Woe to them that call evil good, and good evil; who put darkness for light, and light for darkness."[118] Wrong cannot be permanently enthroned. The stars in their courses fight against all injustice and cruelty and inhumanity. Victory is ever on the side of righteousness. Writing of the battle of Waterloo, Victor Hugo asks: "Was it possible that Napoleon should have won that battle? We answer, No! Why? Because of Wellington? No! Because of Blucher? No!

Because of God!" Let Hugo speak further: "The shadow of a Mighty Hand is cast over Waterloo; it is the day of destiny, and the Force which is above man produced that day. On that day the perspective of the human race was changed, and Waterloo is the hinge of the nineteenth century. The disappearance of the great man was necessary for the advent of a great age, and He to Whom there was no reply, undertook the task!"[119] So was it in 1815. So was it again in 1918. And so shall it be again, please God, in the present ghastly death drama that challenges the world, "for right is right, since God is God, and right the day must win!"[120]

In these difficult and desperate days, it surely behooves us all to fix our thoughts on those "unshakeable things that remain,"[121] as pointed out in the Bible, and to cleave trustfully and obediently to Him Who is "The same yesterday, today and forever."[122] His purposes are as changeless as His own Being, and His righteous will is bound to prevail. "He shall not fail nor be discouraged till He have set justice in the earth."[123] Let us, therefore, courageously face both the present and the future, with the faith that can go alone in the dark, with the love that suffereth long and is kind, and with the commanding and assuring hope voiced by the poet:

> Be Strong!
> It matters not how deeply intrenched the wrong,
> How hard the battle goes, the day how long;
> Faint not—fight on—tomorrow comes the Song![124]

Christmas 1941—New Year 1942

Reflection 33

With the returning Christmas and New Year Season, the perennial reminder of the heaven-sent song of Peace and Good Will to all mankind, let me send you this modest Greeting, voicing every best wish for you and yours, for this happy Season, and beyond, always! Whatever may be your experiences, both for today and for all the unfolding future, I would fervently voice for you the age-old Benediction: "The Lord bless thee and keep thee; the Lord make His face to shine upon thee, and be gracious unto thee; the Lord lift up His countenance upon thee, and give thee peace!"[125]

At this accustomed Season for renewed expressions of friendliness and good will, when old friendships are strengthened and new ones are cemented, let us seek to make such Season more blessed than ever before, by gracious words and helpful deeds, for all those whose lives especially appeal for our understanding and practical sympathy. Included within this circle are the poor and needy; the sick and suffering; the bereaved and sorrowing; the eager children, and the aged, whose steps are feeble and slow. Indeed, let us worthily remember all who are facing heavy odds, and bearing unusual burdens. A poet thus points the way for us:

> For somehow, not only for Christmas,
> But all the long year through,

> The joy that you give to others
> Is the joy that comes back to you:
> And the more that you spend in blessing
> The poor and lonely and sad,
> The more of your hearts possessing
> Returns to make you glad.[126]

Edward Bok tells us in his autobiography that his grandmother gave him the wise admonition: "See to it that you leave the world a little better and a little more beautiful than you found it."[127] The story is told of great-souled Phillips Brooks, that one of his members returned from church, one day, and was asked this question by his mother: "How did Dr. Brooks preach today?" The reply was: "Oh, I have heard Him preach greater sermons, many times, but I think I never realized before how much he loves us." Somebody repeated that to the great preacher, and at once his eyes overflowed with tears as he said: "I would rather have that said about me than anything else."[128] Faithfully does God's Book remind us that, although prophecies shall fail, and tongues shall cease, and knowledge shall vanish away, yet "Love never faileth."[129] Life's burdens are made lighter and better and safer, by the grace of understanding sympathy, in all the relations of life—personal, social, economic, religious, national, and international.

As this Good Will Season returns to us, a Blackout casts its darkening and devastating shadows over the whole earth. In 1914, when the world was plunged into the first World War, Sir Edward Grey uttered these ominous words: "The lamps are going out all over Europe, and they will not be lit again in our life-time."[130] History repeats itself. The lights are still going out, not only in Europe, but throughout the poignantly troubled nations,

large and small. A trail of war and suffering and hunger
and inhuman enslavement is being blazed around the
encircling globe. Two interpretations of life are now ter-
ribly engaged in a global war—Individualism and Totalitarianism. The world-shaking issue confronts humanity
with one of the major crises of all history. The present
immeasurably momentous hour imperiously challenges
the sanest thought and the noblest behavior of all mankind. The founding fathers of our beloved country recog-
nized God as the supreme source of our needed wisdom
and strength, by writing into the declaration of our country's independence, that all men are endowed by their
Creator with certain inalienable rights, especially naming
life, liberty and the pursuit of happiness. Of all the errors
running through the bestialized philosophy of mad dic-
tators, now seeking to scuttle civilization, the most per-
nicious and horrible error is the brazen and blasphemous
contempt for the worth and dignity of human life—of any
and every human life, anywhere and everywhere. All the
great reforms in history have been waged for the rights of
the individual, whether in politics, economics, or religion.

In the present, destiny-determining days, let us make
John Oxenham's words our very own:

> Man proposes, God disposes
> Still our trust in Him reposes,
> Who in war-time still makes roses.[131]

When President Washington was inaugurated as our
first President, he uttered these wisely admonitory words:
"Heaven can never smile on a nation that disregards the
rules of order and right." Surely, it behooves us faithfully to
see to it, in all our programs and progress, that righteousness

is supremely enthroned, everywhere. The downfall of nations comes only when the people fail to listen to God's teachings, and to obey His commands.

Large numbers of our heroic young men and women are now dedicating their lives to defend, and to build a better civilization. Let them be enshrined in our unceasing and most fervent prayers, that they may ever be guided and kept by the Friend that sticketh closer than a brother; and that God will, in His own time and way, make an end of tyrannies, granting victory to the cause of righteousness and freedom, everywhere! Lord Nelson's prayer for his country and her defenders, before Trafalgar, may well be our unceasing prayer for our country and her defenders: "May the Great God Whom I serve, grant to my country a great and glorious victory, and may no misconduct in any way tarnish it. To God I entrust the just cause it is given me to defend!"

In one of the supremely decisive hours in the life of Robert Louis Stevenson, he gives this personal testimony: "I came about like a well-handled ship. There stood at the wheel that unknown Oarsman whom we call God."[132] Here then is the supreme fact in life: "The Lord God omnipotent reigneth." Because of the character and the purposes of God, let us put away all doubt as to the ultimate triumph of righteousness throughout all the earth.

As we turn from another passing year to the dawning New Year, may we wisely leave behind all that would mar our peace and progress, and carry forward only that which would make life happier and better for ourselves and others. May there be such unity in our purposes as shall blend the temporal and spiritual in such a way as to glorify the whole life. If some days shall be marked by prosperity and others by adversity, may we not be coarsened by the one nor embittered by the other. May we be lifted above the pessimism which magnifies the shadows, and be fortified by the optimism which sees the way of life as the shining light which shineth more and more unto the Perfect Day.

Christmas 1942—New Year 1943

Reflection 34

The wistful and mystic Christmas and New Year Season is again with us, when expressions of love and good will are given renewed and deepened emphasis, in all the relations of life. In such Season, let me voice for you and yours, all that is highest and best in the age-old greeting: "A Merry Christmas and a Happy New Year." Let us especially seek, by timely words and heart-cheering deeds, to make the Season all that it ought to be, for the eager young people, and for those whose steps are slow, and whose strength is waning; for those who watch and wait and weep; for those who keep punctual tryst with grief and watchful visit with pain; for those who feel the biting sting of disappointment, and, indeed, for those of every age who may be facing heavy odds and bearing unusual burdens. A poet thus points the way for us:

> On the sad and the lonely, the troubled and poor,
> The voice of the Christ-child shall fall;
> And to every blind wanderer open the door
> Of a hope he had not dreamed of before,
> With a sunshine and welcome for all.[133]

This "Good Will Season" is the season of the open heart, when home loves and loyalties and right standards are more consciously made real to us, and more affectionately appraised by us, than in the usual days. Well may it be so, for as goes the home, so shall go all else throughout the entire social order. Likewise, at this Season, we are made to realize afresh, the healing, inspiring power of friendship, and the measureless joy and blessing we have in our friends. It is said that Elizabeth Browning once asked Charles Kingsley: "Tell me the secret of your victorious life, that I may know how to make my life beautiful." His brief reply was: "I had a friend."[134] And Robert Louis Stevenson said: "So long as we love, we serve. So long as we are loved by others, I would almost say that we are indispensable." The late nobly gifted, widely useful Dr. William Lyon Phelps of Yale University, makes this very revealing remark in his autobiography: "Perhaps the chief source of my happiness is the gift of appreciation." The Bible tells us two vital things about our friends and friendships: "A friend loveth at all times"; and "A man that hath friends must show himself friendly."[135] The whole structure of the world will be changed by the worthy practice of the right kind of friendship.

Again, the joyous Christmas Season returns to us in a day when the world is war-torn, blood-drenched and menaced with anxieties, atrocities and sufferings too terrible for words. It is a global War, in which whole nations are being oppressed and destroyed, while both sorrow and death are riding roughshod over millions of men, women and little children. It is a War where two ideologies are in mortal combat—democracy and autocracy, freedom and tyranny. Liberty-loving people cannot, dare not be indifferent to the amazing and worldwide efforts to subjugate and enslave humanity, everywhere. The two ideas in the awful conflict are as far apart as the poles. One view supremely magnifies the dignity and value and indefeasible rights of the individual, any and everywhere. The other view denies the dignity and value of the individual, and appraises him merely as a cog in a machine.

At this Season, our hearts go out in untold gratitude and most fervent prayers, for our grandly heroic men and women, in the armed service of their country, and for the highest welfare of humanity, both for today and tomorrow. They are the answer to this prayer:

> God send us men with hearts ablaze,
> All truth to love, all wrong to hate;
> These are the patriots nations need,
> These are the bulwarks of the State.[136]

They have gone forth, highly resolved to pay the full price to insure the matchless blessings of liberty, for ourselves, and for the whole world. Their high behavior challenges the admiration of liberty-loving peoples, everywhere. Surely, it should be an invincible appeal to the people at the home front to "carry on" at the highest and best, in home and church and state. The supreme test of life is not how long any of us may live, but how much and how well do we live. Well does Rudyard Kipling remind us: "A man may be festooned with the whole haberdashery of success, and go to his grave a castaway."[137] When John Bunyan was offered his freedom from prison, if he would keep silent concerning his convictions, he made the sublime reply: "I'll tarry in prison till the moss grows on my eyebrows ere I make a slaughterhouse of my conscience, or a butchery of my principles." Fidelity to duty, whatever the cost, is success at the highest.

As we face the stress and strain of the awful war, let us see faithfully all along to the motives that actuate our lives. One of the greatest soldiers of all time was General Robert E. Lee. These are his lofty words: "I have never cherished toward the Northern people bitter and vindictive feelings, and have never seen the day when I did not pray for them." In like spirit spoke President Lincoln, in his Second Inaugural: "With malice toward none, with charity for all." China's first lady, Madam Chiang Kai-Shek, said recently: "No matter what we have undergone and suffered, we must try to forgive those who injure us, and remember only the lesson gained thereby. Christ taught us to hate the evil in men, but not men themselves." It is glorious to hear that our soldiers are magnifying the patriotism that reveres God and seeks to follow where He leads.

On every hand the question is unceasingly echoed: "What of the outcome of this global War?" One of our lads, as he left home for training as an army pilot, in one of America's airfields, sublimely said: "I don't know *what* the future holds, but I know *who* holds the future." Because of the character and invincible purpose of God, we need not have one doubt of the ultimate triumph of righteousness in this War, and beyond, always.

> This is my Father's world,
> The battle is not done,
> Jesus who died shall be satisfied,
> And earth and heaven be one.
>
> This is my Father's world,
> Why should my heart be sad?
> The Lord is King, let the heavens ring;
> God reigns, let the earth be glad.[138]

Christmas 1943—New Year 1944

A Benediction

Over the course of his ministry, Truett would conclude Sunday evening services with the benediction printed below. It seems a most suitable way to conclude a volume where ends give rise and way to beginnings.

And now as the people go their many scattered ways,

May the blessings of God,
Bright like the light when the morning dawneth

And gracious as the dew when the evening-tide cometh,

Be granted you, all and each,
Now and forevermore.[139]

Notes

1   Established in 1991, Baylor University's George W. Truett Seminary began offering classes in 1994. Meanwhile, the university into which the seminary is embedded was founded in 1845 and is the oldest continuously operating university in the state of Texas, as well as one of the first educational institutions west of the Mississippi River.

2   See, however, Keith E. Durso, *Thy Will Be Done: A Biography of George W. Truett* (Macon, Ga.: Mercer Academic Press, 2009). Note also Powhatan W. James, *George W. Truett: A Biography* (New York: Macmillan, 1939).

3   Southern Baptist minister Dr. I. J. Van Ness (1861–1947), a Baylor graduate who worked at the Baptist Sunday School from 1900 to 1935, composed an introduction to the first volume of Dr. Truett's year-end messages written for his congregation. Published by Richard R. Smith, Inc. of New York in 1929 under the title *These Gracious Years*, the book begins with Truett's 1910 Christmas message to his people and concludes with his 1928–1929 end-of-the-year address.

4   See Revelation 21:4, 23.

5   This lyrical line inspired this volume's title.

6   Although not placed in quotation marks, the phrase a "friend speaketh to a friend" is drawn from Exodus 33:11 (KJV).

7   Informed, in part, by the Gospel of John, Truett sometimes refers to Jesus as "Friend" (see esp. John 15:15). On having not seen Christ, note, e.g., 1 Peter 1:8.

8   The words in quotations are drawn from the third stanza of the hymn "Lead, Kindly Light" (Words: John Henry Newman, 1801–1890; Music: John B. Dykes, 1823–1876).

9   Reverberations of John 14:1-4 may be heard both here and elsewhere in Truett's closing lines.

10   Mark 10:45 ("The Son of Man did not come to be served, but to serve and to give his life as a ransom for many") punctuated Truett's messages and animated Truett's ministry.

11   Note Ecclesiastes 3:11, where it states that God has "set eternity in the human heart."

12   On the "crown of life" in Scripture, see James 1:12 and Revelation 2:12.

13   While the first, this will by no means be the last reference that Truett makes in his various messages to Luke's nativity story in general (esp. Luke 2:8-14) and to the heavenly hosts' *Gloria in Excelsis* in particular (Luke 2:13).

14   Truett composed these lines in the midst of World War I (1914–1918), citing lines from Isaiah 2:4 // Micah 4:3: "[T]hey shall beat their swords into plowshares, and their spears into pruning hooks. . . ."

15   Cf. the concluding line of Simeon's *Nunc Dimittis* in Luke 2:35.

16   The line "trace the rainbow through the rain" is drawn from the third stanza of the hymn "O Love, that wilt not let me go" (Words: George Matheson, 1842–1906; Lyrics: Albert Lister Peace, 1844–1912).

17   World War I ended on November 11, 1918 and was followed by the signing of various treaties in subsequent years.

18   The turning of water into wine refers, of course, to Jesus' first recorded miracle in John's Gospel—his changing water into wine at a wedding feast in Cana of Galilee. See John 2:1-12.

19   The parable of the Good Samaritan is recorded in Luke 10:25-37. Acts 10:38 speaks of Jesus as one who "went about doing good."

20   Truett was preaching among the Allied forces in World War I at this time.

21   Compare Paul's description of love in 1 Corinthians 13:4-7.

22   Truett is referring here to World War I.

23   So Luke 22:27.

24   See Ephesians 1:14.

25   See Proverbs 18:24.

26   Echoes of Romans 5:8 and 1 Corinthians 15:56 are detectable in the latter part of this expansive sentence.

27   Another partial citation of the hymn "O Love, that wilt not let me go" (Words: George Matheson, 1842–1906; Lyrics: Albert Lister Peace, 1844–1912).

28   On the "pillar of cloud by day and the pillar of fire by night," see Exodus 13:21. On Jesus as "the way, the truth, and the life," see John 14:6.

29 Recall Matthew 5:9a: "Blessed are the peacemakers . . . ."

30 The figure of the "Grim Reaper," representing death, appears to have arisen in Europe in the fourteenth century during the time of a pandemic known as the Black Death.

31 For the biblical story of "the tower of Babel," see Genesis 11:1-9.

32 See John 10:10.

33 The so-called Golden Rule is found in Matthew 7:12: "Do unto others as you would have them do unto you."

34 This sentence is informed by the story of Jesus' transfiguration recorded in Synoptic Gospels (see Matthew 17:1-21; Mark 9:2-29; Luke 9:28-43).

35 See Romans 8:39.

36 Proverbs 13:12 maintains that "hope deferred makes the heart sick."

37 Quoting Luke 22:37, while alluding to 1 Peter 2:21.

38 An allusion to Psalm 80:5.

39 This succinct preface was written by George W. Truett's wife, Josephine Jenkins Truett, whom he met at Baylor and married on June 28, 1894. At the time of Truett's death (July 7, 1944), they had been married a little over fifty years. The Truetts, both Baylor graduates, had three children together, all daughters. The volume *Christmas Messages*, published by Moody Press in 1945, contained the last fifteen year-end messages that Truett composed, the final of which was written from his sickbed in December 1943.

40 The Greek mythological figure Tantalus was perpetually punished in Tartarus. He was consigned to stand in a pool of water beneath a fruit tree, without being able to reach and thereby eat of its fruit and without being able to drink of the always-receding water.

41 See Matthew 10:29-31.

42 Note Colossians 2:3.

43 Truett is referring, of course, to the secluded glen of Sleepy Hollow that features in Washington Irving's gothic story "The Legend of Sleepy Hollow." It is readily apparent throughout Truett's messages, in print and otherwise, that he was a lover of literature. Sources suggest that his only hobby was book collecting and that he had over ten thousand volumes in his personal library.

44 See Psalm 90:12.

45 On the gifts of the magi, see Matthew 2:11.

46 On eating the "bread of sorrow," see Psalm 127:2.

47 The quote is from a poem written by Robert Browning (1812–1889).

48 Mark 9:35; 10:44

49   See Matthew 7:26.

50   A reference to Jesus' parable of the Good Samaritan. See Luke 10:30-35, esp. 10:30.

51   Isaiah 30:21

52   See Joshua 7:26; Isaiah 65:10; Hosea 2:15.

53   Proverbs 27:10

54   See Matthew 2:2.

55   Psalm 90:12

56   Note again 1 Corinthians 13:4-8a.

57   This statement, frequently attributed to James Matthew Barrie (1860–1937), the creator of Peter Pan, appears in the first paragraph in his essay entitled "Courage." See https://www.online -literature.com/barrie/2088/.

58   This sentence alludes to Ecclesiastes 11:1.

59   The story of the legendary city of Atlantis first appears in Plato's *Timaeus*.

60   See Jeremiah 2:13; John 4:14; 7:38-39.

61   Note Psalm 23:4.

62   This Christmas greeting was sent while Truett was touring mission fields in 1935–1936 while serving as President of the Baptist World Alliance (1934–1939).

63   Robert H. Coleman was Truett's beloved, long-time associate at First Baptist Church, Dallas, Texas. Coleman is also remembered as a publisher of hymnals.

64   The phrase "word of the cross" is drawn from 1 Corinthians 1:18.

65   John 15:5

66   Ephesians 6:24

67   An apparent reference to Karl Marx's contention that "religion . . . is the opiate of the masses" ("Die Religion . . . ist das Opium des Volkes")

68   Matthew 5:16

69   Luke 12:15

70   John 16:8

71   See Galatians 5:22.

72   1 Corinthians 15:25; cf. Psalm 8:6.

73   See Colossians 2:7.

74   Note Ephesians 3:8.

75   "Tiny Tim" is a character in Charles Dickens' *A Christmas Carol*, who makes the statement that Truett quotes as a blessing at Christmas dinner. Dickens repeats the line at the conclusion of the story.

76   From John Greenleaf Whittier's "A Christmas Carmen" (1894).

77   World War II would commence on September 1, 1939.

78 Referring to World War I, which lasted from 1914 to 1918.

79 Luke 2:11

80 Isaiah 9:6

81 Note 1 Timothy 2:5.

82 1 Corinthians 13:8

83 Luke 2:10-11

84 Luke 2:12

85 Psalm 46:10

86 2 Corinthians 5:19

87 See Philippians 4:7.

88 A reference to Herod the Great, who was ruling as a Roman client king over Judea when Jesus was born (73–4 BC; ruled 37–4 BC).

89 For quotes such as this from Napoleon Bonaparte (1769–1821), emperor of France, see further John S. C. Abbott, *Confidential Correspondence of the Emperor Napoleon and the Empress Josephine* (New York: Mason Brothers, 1856).

90 1 Corinthians 15:25

91 Psalm 30:5

92 1 Corinthians 15:57

93 Bertel Thorwaldsen (1770–1844) was a famed Danish sculptor who spent most of his life in Italy.

94 Rudyard Kipling (1865–1936) was a well-known English writer born in India. This line is drawn from his poem "A Song in Storm."

95 Dan Crawford (1870–1926) was a Scottish-born Bible translator and missionary to Central Africa. In the year of his death, Crawford adopted the line Truett quotes as his motto.

96 This line is drawn from Rupert Brooke's poem "August 1914." Brooke (1887–1915) was an English poet who died an early death during World War I.

97 Matthew 25:40

98 See Reflection 25 above.

99 Charles Lamb (1775–1834) was an English writer.

100 Philippians 3:13

101 Robert Louis Stevenson (1850–1894) was a Scottish novelist and travel writer. The line Truett quotes is drawn from Stevenson's essay entitled "An Apology for Idlers."

102 In Revelation 19:6, this declaration is made by a great heavenly multitude.

103 The second half of this sentence is drawn from Psalm 89:14.

104 This line is from the poem of James Russell Lowell (1819–1891), an American Romantic poet, entitled "The Present Crisis."

105 The statue to which Truett refers is known as Christ the Redeemer of the Andes, which was unveiled on March 13, 1904.

106 The lines Truett quotes are from the poem by American poet Henry Wadsworth Longfellow (1807–1882) entitled "Christmas Day." The familiar Christmas carol "I Heard the Bells on Christmas Day" is based upon Longfellow's poem.

107 These words are commonly attributed to, though not certainly attributable to, George Washington (1732–1799), the first president of the United States (served 1789–1797). George Truett's middle name was "Washington."

108 Woodrow Wilson (1857–1924) served as the twenty-eighth president of the United States from 1913 to 1921.

109 These lines form the last stanza of the poem "In Memoriam" by British poet Alfred Lord Tennyson (1809–1892).

110 Luke 2:10-11, 14

111 Isaiah 41:6

112 This anonymous poem is entitled "Did You Give Him a Lift?"

113 Drawn from Ralph Waldo Emerson's poem "Sacrifice." Emerson (1803–1882) was an American writer, lecturer, philosopher, and poet of the nineteenth century.

114 See Psalm 137.

115 These are the first lines of Brooke's poem entitled "The Soldier."

116 Proverbs 14:34

117 Micah 6:8

118 Isaiah 5:20

119 Truett quotes these lines from Hugo's 1862 novel *Les Misérables*. Victor Marie Hugo (1802–1885) was a French literary artist.

120 These are lines from the final stanza of the Frederick William Faber (1814–1863) poem "The Right Must Win." Faber was an English theologian and hymn writer.

121 Hebrews 12:27

122 Hebrews 13:8

123 Isaiah 42:4

124 From the last stanza of the hymn "Be Strong" (Words: Maltbie D. Babcock, 1858–1901; Music: Carl F. Price, 1881–1948).

125 Numbers 6:24-26

126 This short poem, entitled "Somehow not only for Christmas," was composed by American poet John Greenleaf Whittier (1807–1892).

127 Edward Bok (1863–1930) was an American editor and author who was born in the Netherlands.

128 Phillips Brooks (1835–1893), who wrote the Christmas carol "O Little Town of Bethlehem," was an American Episcopal minister and author.

129 Luke 2 is the only text to which Truett refers more frequently in his year-end messages than 1 Corinthians 13.

130 This statement was made by British Foreign Secretary Sir Edward Grey on August 3, 1914, as the United Kingdom entered into World War I, and is preserved in Grey's personal memoirs.

131 John Oxenham was (one of) the pen name(s) of the English literary artist William Arthur Dunkerly (1852–1941). These lines appear in Oxenham's poem "Here, There, and Everywhere."

132 A similar statement may be found in Graham Balfour's *The Life of Robert Louis Stevenson* (2 vols.; New York: Charles Scribner's Sons, 1901), 1:122.

133 The third stanza of a Phillips Brooks Christmas carol entitled "The Voice of the Christ Child."

134 Elizabeth Barrett Browning (1806–1861) was an English poet of the Victorian era. Charles Kingsley (1819–1875) was, among other things, an Anglican priest.

135 Proverbs 17:17; 18:24

136 The third and final stanza of a hymn entitled "God Send Us Men Whose Aim 'Twill Be" (Words: Frederick J. Gillman, 1866–1949).

137 Drawn from an address delivered by Kipling entitled "Independence."

138 It is altogether fitting that Truett would conclude what proved to be his final year-end message by quoting a stanza of a Maltbie Babcock poem, "My Father's World."

139 Longtime Baylor history professor Dr. James W. Vardaman, now deceased (1928–2018), grew up under the pastoral ministry of Truett at First Baptist Church, Dallas. It was a profound, memorable moment when Dr. Vardaman pronounced Truett's Sunday evening benediction over the summer 2017 graduating class of our seminary. This volume is dedicated to his memory and to all who have been and will be impacted by the ministry of George W. Truett and those ministers associated with the school that bears his good name.